The HARLEM HELLFIGHTERS

WHEN PRIDE MET COURAGE

Walter Dean Myers
and Bill Miles

HarperCollins*Publishers*

Pictured above: Croix de Guerre

Photo credits:
Title page: Courtesy of Bill Miles
Pages 13, 21, 23, 42, 46, 47 (top), 57, 60–61 (top), 64, 65 (both), 68–69, 76–77, 85, 86, 87, 88, 92–93 (both), 98, 101, 104, 111, 116–117, 135, 136–137, 138 (both), 139, 140, 141, 142, 144, 146, 151 are courtesy of National Archives
Page 50-52: Courtesy of Moorland-Spingarn Research Center, Howard University
Page 130–31 top: Courtesy of Ann and Jeni Estill
All other images are from the Walter Dean Myers Archives

The Harlem Hellfighters: When Pride Met Courage

Library of Congress Cataloging-in-Publication Data
Myers, Walter Dean, date
    The Harlem Hellfighters : when pride met courage / Walter Dean Myers and Bill Miles.— 1st ed.
        p.   cm.
    Summary: The true story of the African American heroes of World War I, the soldiers of the 369th Infantry Regiment, dubbed the "Harlem Hellfighters."
    ISBN-10: 0-06-001136-X—ISBN-10: 0-06-001137-8 (lib. bdg.)
    ISBN-13: 978-0-06-001136-9—ISBN-13: 978-0-06-001137-6 (lib. bdg.)
    1. United States. Army. Infantry Regiment, 369th—Juvenile literature. 2. World War, 1914–1918—Participation, African American—Juvenile literature. 3. United States. Army—African American troops—Juvenile literature. 4. African Americans—Social conditions—To 1964—Juvenile literature. I. Miles, William, date. II. Title.
D570.33 369th .M94 2006
[940.4'1273'08996073]—dc22   2005008951
                                                                          CIP
                                                                          AC

Typography by Carla Weise
1 2 3 4 5 6 7 8 9 10
❖
First Edition

PREFACE

As a child growing up in Harlem, I enjoyed life to the fullest. During the summers I played ball in the streets and dove off the old piers into the East River. On the way to the piers I noticed the large, formidable building that was the armory. I had only a vague idea of what I wanted to do as an adult. But one warm day a bit of a miracle occurred. That miracle was the marching band of the 369th Infantry Regiment.

I heard the steady beat of the drums and the call of the brass echoing against the redbrick tenements and rushed with a group of friends to see what was going on. What I saw were black soldiers in company formation. The men stood tall in perfect lines across the wide avenue. Their uniforms were neatly pressed, and the sun glistened off the rifles they carried slung over their shoulders.

An officer gave an order and the soldiers stepped out, all on the left foot, all in perfect rhythm. There was an obvious pride in the marching, in the crisp responses to commands. I wasn't sure what I felt, but I knew I wanted to march with them, to be a part of this magnificent array. On June 26, 1948, I joined the 369th, known as the "Harlem Hellfighters."

As I learned more about the regiment, I realized that the pride I had felt when I first saw it was becoming an important part of who

I was. The 369th was not only an outstanding military unit; it also represented a part of the history of my Harlem community and, as such, part of my history as well. As I learned the story of the regiment—how it was first formed, its glorious record in World War I—I knew I was discovering a hidden history of African American accomplishments.

In the 369th I found a brotherhood of soldiers whose bravery and dedication brought them respect and admiration that were often denied outside the military experience. Judging by what I felt when I put on the uniform and marched or trained with the 369th, I could easily understand how the men who had first joined the old 15th New York National Guard back in 1916 felt.

The 15th, which became the 369th, faced prejudice and segregation but endured to perform valiantly. When, in 1917, President Woodrow Wilson declared that America was entering the war to make the world "safe for democracy," many questioned why African Americans, routinely segregated and often abused, would voluntarily enter the armed forces, risking their lives for a country that had not yet afforded them equal rights. The answer to that question lies in the story of the 369th. Men such as James Reese Europe, Horace Pippin, Henry Johnson, and Robert Needham defined the identity of African Americans by their bravery and their dedication. Hundreds of black men laid down their lives in France because they refused to believe that they were anything but men, worthy of being Americans and representing their country.

As unit historian I recognize that the documentation of the 369th is as vital to understanding the African American experience as any story about slavery or the civil rights movement. For in the story of the 369th—in the trenches of France, in the battles of Meuse-Argonne, and at the bloody siege of Sechault—we have African Americans defining their own characters with courage and determination, writing their own history in sweat and blood.

We cannot let this history die, nor can we let it fade away. As it has filled me with pride and given me understanding of one group of outstanding soldiers, so it should be passed on to all Americans to appreciate and honor.

Bill Miles, unit historian

This book is dedicated to all the men and women
who served in the 369th Harlem Hellfighters.
—WDM and BM

A Harlem Hellfighter

CONTENTS

DEFENDING AMERICA

Blacks have participated in all of America's battles. When the first Africans arrived in North America in 1619 as captive labor, they found a conflict between the white British and the Native Americans, who were here first. The colonists were hesitant to arm the very people they had enslaved, but blacks soon found themselves not only working the land but defending it as well. Later, during the French and Indian War (1754–1763), blacks were again called upon to help defend the British.

When the American colonies declared their independence on July 4, 1776, thousands of blacks lived in the thirteen colonies. Most of them were slaves. Some were promised their freedom if they fought against the British; others were simply sent into the war as laborers, personal aides, or soldiers. The small American navy consisted largely of privately owned vessels called privateers, and many of these had black

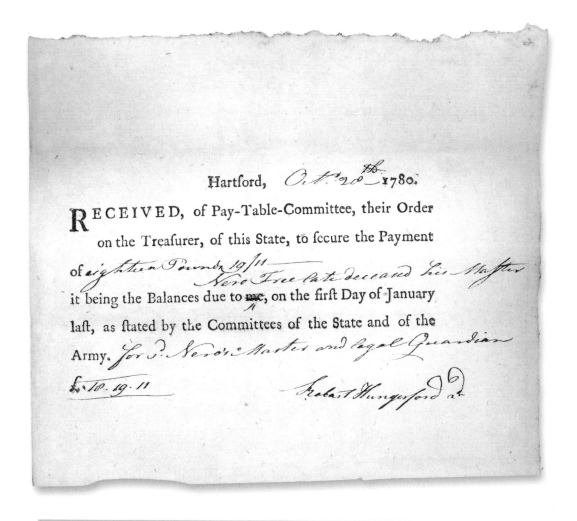

Hartford, Oct 20th 1780.

RECEIVED, of Pay-Table-Committee, their Order on the Treasurer, of this State, to secure the Payment of *eighteen Pounds 19/11* *Nero Free late deceased his Master* it being the Balances due to ~~me~~, on the first Day of January last, as stated by the Committees of the State and of the Army. *for d. Nero's Master and legal Guardian*

£. *10. 19. 11*

Robert Hungerford a.

Pay voucher for Nero Free, a dead black Revolutionary soldier—the money going to his master

sailors among them. James Forten, a free black youth of fourteen living in Philadelphia, sailed with Captain Stephen Decatur Sr. aboard the *Royal Louis* in the summer of 1781. The first voyage of the *Royal Louis* resulted in a stunning victory against a British ship and the taking of the ship as a prize of war. Forten's luck did not last very long, and the

Royal Louis was captured by a British warship. Forten, who had befriended the son of the captain who held him, refused the chance to go over to the British side and escape imprisonment. He saw himself, even during this period in which slavery was legal, as an American and remained loyal to the American cause.

Eventually, more than five thousand black men would fight for the independence of the colonies. A Hessian soldier commented in his diary that there were blacks in every American regiment that he had seen.

During the course of the war the British offered freedom to any slave who would fight with the British against the colonists. Many blacks did escape to the British lines and either worked as laborers for the British or participated in battles against the rebellious Americans.

During the Revolutionary War the colonists were divided in the treatment of black men. On one hand they were being asked to fight for the liberation of the colonies, but on the other hand they were not being guaranteed their own freedom. Lord Dunmore, the governor of the Virginia Colony and a British loyalist, had worried about the presence of blacks in Virginia. He felt that the blacks would side with whoever offered them freedom. When the war began, he offered blacks their freedom in return for fighting with the British. Hundreds of black men joined the British army and fought against America, sometimes having to fight against the many thousands of blacks who fought for the colonists.

The war ended successfully for the colonists, and many slaves who had taken up arms or labored for the Americans were recognized and given their freedom in thanks for their participation in the war. Blacks who fought for the British were, by agreement between the American and British governments, given their freedom and taken to the West Indies or to Canada after the war.

Most of the battles in the War of 1812 against Great Britain took place at sea with mixed crews of blacks and whites. General Andrew Jackson, fighting off the British at the end of the war, put out a call to black citizens to fight in the American army: "Through a mistaken policy you have heretofore been deprived of a participation in the glorious struggle for national rights in which our country is engaged. This no longer shall exist."

Black soldiers served in this brief war both as soldiers and as laborers, building fortifications, carrying supplies, and even acting as spies.

The United States of America is a constitutional democracy guaranteeing its citizens certain rights. During the period of American slavery these rights were not being given to black people. Throughout early American history there have been incidents in which black people revolted against those who would keep them in slavery.

In 1822 a free black, Denmark Vesey, planned a slave revolt in Charleston, South Carolina. In 1831 Nat Turner led an armed rebellion that ended with the deaths of more than fifty whites. In 1839 Africans aboard the ship *Amistad* killed the Spanish crew and

LOOK OUT FOR PRIZE MONEY.

WANTED, MEN FOR THE NAVY,
                    WHITE OR COLORED.

Apply at 509 New Jersey avenue.   jy27-12t*

Civil War newspaper ad for white and colored sailors

captured the vessel. These revolts demonstrated that black people wanted freedom as much as anyone and were willing to fight for it. Recognizing that black people wanted to be free and would do what was necessary to achieve that freedom, slaveholders made it illegal for any black person to be in possession of a firearm, or for blacks to gather in large groups away from the plantations on which they worked. Free blacks were not allowed to travel in Southern states, where most of the slavery existed.

By 1859 the Northern states had developed quite differently than those in the South. The Southern states were primarily agricultural and largely dependent on slave labor for economic success. The Northern states had a mixed economy, with a growing reliance on industry. *Niles' Register*, a nineteenth-century publication that often reflected Southern views, complained that if a Southerner died, he would be buried in a grave dug by a shovel manufactured in the North, buried in a casket made in the North, and preached over by a minister holding a Bible printed in the North.

For young Southerners who did not want to be planters, the military became the pathway to becoming "an officer and a gentleman." A large number of the officers in the American army were from the slave states of the South. On October 16, 1859, they would be tested both as soldiers and as Southerners.

Harper's Ferry, Virginia, was a small, somewhat sleepy town with little to distinguish it from the neighboring areas except for its military arsenal. It was this arsenal that was the target of John Brown and the black and white raiders with him. Brown's object was to break into the arsenal, take as many guns as possible, and hide them in the surrounding mountains. He then planned to put out a call for the slaves in the area to begin a rebellion. Robert E. Lee led a group of Marines to Harper's Ferry to put down the disturbance. Brown was captured, and he and the survivors of the raid were tried and executed.

But the differences between North and South, free states and slave states, grew to be too difficult to overcome, and within eighteen months of Brown's raid the country was embroiled in the Civil War.

Frederick Douglass, a free black man and an outspoken abolitionist, pleaded with President Abraham Lincoln to allow blacks to fight against the Confederacy: "A war undertaken and brazenly carried on for the perpetual enslavement of colored men, calls logically and loudly for colored men to help suppress it."

Both Douglass and Lincoln sensed that the war would bring an

E Company, 9th Cavalry, known as Buffalo Soldiers

end to American slavery. Douglass knew that if blacks had no part in a Northern victory, they would have little claim to the moral high ground in the postwar period.

Lincoln was hesitant. He knew that Southerners would be particularly bitter if he armed black soldiers. But eventually, black soldiers were needed and a Union general assembled the 1st South Carolina Colored Volunteers. Other "colored troops," including the 54th Regiment of Massachusetts Volunteers of African Descent, were also

Training at Camp Upton, New York

created. In all, 180,000 black men fought in the war and helped to defeat the Confederacy.

After the Civil War the United States government authorized the creation of a limited number of black military units. From this handful of black units emerged the 24th and 25th Infantry Regiments and the 9th and 10th Cavalry Regiments. These units were primarily assigned to duties in the rugged western states. They were most often in areas in which Native Americans were being forced onto reservations. Because of their woolly hair they were called Buffalo Soldiers by the Native Americans.

During the Spanish-American War (1898) black soldiers were sent to Cuba to fight with the Cubans against the Spanish. Then, in 1899, black soldiers were sent to the Philippines to help put down an insurrection there. In both Cuba and the Philippines the black American troops made significant contributions to American victories.

America had fought for and won its independence with the help of black men. The Union army had defeated the Confederacy using black men in its ranks. The United States has also fought minor wars on the sea and in foreign lands using black soldiers. But in each of its conflicts the shadow of race loomed large. It would do so again in what was to become known as the Great War.

WAR IN EUROPE

There are many reasons for wars, most of them reflections of human failures. Countries are invaded, cities and buildings destroyed, and people killed because of political ambitions, greed, or a lust for power. Often wars are caused by too great a willingness to believe that a military plan, no matter how carefully drawn, cannot fail.

Borders within Europe had changed many times in the two hundred years prior to 1914. Great Britain, with its vastly superior navy, expanded in the seventeenth and eighteenth centuries to establish colonies in North America and Australia. It lost an important part of its North American colonies during the Revolutionary War, but during the War of 1812 it successfully defended its Canadian colony. By the 1820s Great Britain had begun establishing colonies in southern Africa and Asia. By 1858 the British controlled what are now India, Pakistan, Bangladesh, Myanmar, and Sri Lanka. As the nineteenth century drew to a close, many European nations believed they had the right to control the less technically advanced areas of the world. A mad scramble for colonies began as countries vied to increase their worldwide influence. They also wanted to control as many of the natural resources and wealth as possible.

In 1884 the strongest nations of Europe, most notably England, Germany, Belgium, and France, gathered in Berlin to solidify their territorial claims in Africa.

The growing wealth of the European powers was accompanied by great advancements in technology. By the end of the nineteenth century, the automobile had been invented, and in 1903 the Wright brothers had made their famous flight at Kitty Hawk, North Carolina. Marine technology—the building of powerful, well-armed ships—was also advancing, as was the development of the arms industry. Perhaps the most significant technical advances were in railroad technology. Vast numbers of people and quantities of material could be transported long distances in a relatively short period of time.

Between 1904 and 1914 Germany became very aggressive in its territorial challenges on the European continent. During the Franco-Prussian War (1870–1871) France had lost a great deal of territory to the emerging nation-state of Germany. Now Germany, along with its ally Austria-Hungary, was threatening to advance even more into neighboring countries.

Britain, France, and Russia made hasty treaties trying to counter the German threat. It was clear that not only was Germany determined to become the most powerful European nation, but it also wanted a world role and would use its military strength to achieve it. German ships were large, and their big guns were superior to anything the French and British had. Germany had a well-trained army, while the British were still depending on volunteers.

Alliances were formed and treaties were signed all over the world. Nations thousands of miles apart, many without armies, agreed to side either with the Germans and Austro-Hungarians or with the British, French, and Russian alliance.

After years of provocative diplomacy, politely exchanged insults, and thinly veiled threats, all that was needed for a war was an excuse. The excuse came on June 28, 1914.

Austrian Archduke Francis Ferdinand and his wife, Sophie, were in Sarajevo, Bosnia, which was then under the uneasy control of Austria-Hungary. The local people, the Serbs, resented the control by Austria-Hungary as well as the military exercise that the archduke was about to direct. A young Serbian man, nineteen-year-old Gavrilo Princip, shot and killed the archduke and his wife to protest the Austrian presence in his country. First Austria-Hungary made demands that it knew Serbia would reject; then it declared war on the small country.

Serbia had made a pact of mutual defense with France, so the possibility of the war spreading became immediate. Great Britain tried to negotiate a settlement, but there was no real interest on the part of

German ship Scharnhorst

Austria-Hungary. Germany, in support of Austria-Hungary but really advancing its own aims, declared war on France and demanded passage through Belgium to stage the attack. Belgium refused, so Germany and Austria-Hungary declared war on Belgium. Soon nations that were colonies of other nations, or allies, or even trading partners, were declaring war. The "war to end all wars" had begun.

German military commanders had planned for just such a war and thought it would be over within months. They had the best technology and the best soldiers, and they thought they had a plan that would defeat France within weeks and establish the German state as the dominant one in western Europe. Then they would turn eastward to Russia.

The United States, on the far side of the Atlantic, was not considered a major power at the outset of the war. It had only a small army and no apparent interests to be considered in Europe. Woodrow Wilson, the president, had publicly opposed any American participation in the war.

TRENCH WARFARE

The war in Europe began with an aggressive attack by Germany and Austria-Hungary, the Central Powers. German troops moved quickly through Belgium, violating that country's neutrality and bringing Great Britain into the war. The advance was so rapid that it became somewhat disorganized, elements of the German army lost contact with their supply lines, and the plans for a massive push became bogged down. Still, the Germans hoped to end the war quickly. But once the initial thrust into Belgium and northern France had slowed and soldiers were in stationary positions waiting for their supply lines to catch up with them, advancement became extremely difficult. The major reason was the very technology of modern warfare that had made Germany superior.

In previous wars the major weapon had been the rifle. With most rifles a good soldier could fire between five and ten aimed shots per minute. But with a machine gun, the new technology, he could fire well over two hundred shots per minute. This made the conventional attack, with men charging over a battlefield, an impossibility. Any attacking force could be stopped with well-placed machine-gun fire. An attack by the British on a German position along the Somme River in northern France produced sixty thousand British casualties—men either killed or wounded—in a single day.

The Great War soon became the bloodiest conflict known to human experience. No amount of bravery could overcome the technology of the machine gun or the newly developed artillery that sent shells traveling from miles behind the front line into the enemy ranks. The use of modern technology was not consistent at the beginning of the war. While it's hard to imagine in this modern age, the onset of the war actually saw soldiers on horseback, their sabers drawn, charging into ranks of armored vehicles and rapid-firing light weapons.

Tank warfare, although deadly against ground soldiers, was too primitive to overcome the most dominant feature of the war, the defensive trench. Both the German army and the Allies built trenches, six to fourteen feet deep, to protect their soldiers. A typical trench complex—and some were very complex indeed—consisted of several rows of dugout earthworks. They would zigzag for miles across the terrain that was being defended. The most forward dugout would be the firing trench, from which men would fire on the enemy. There would be passages from the firing trench to a

Right: Trench interior

Below: Aerial view of French trenches

more securely built covered trench. Behind this trench there would be another trench, where supplies were kept and where the wounded would be taken. Then there might be yet another trench in which men not engaged in the fighting would be on reserve. In between the trenches there would be barbed wire, mines, and sandbags.

While the Germans built such a series of trenches to protect a territory they had already taken, the Allies built their own trenches to prevent the Germans from advancing farther. A line of trenches was dug all across France, where most of the Great War took place. The trenches were often close enough for the men on both sides to see and hear one another, for shaking a fist, or for a

Trench and barbed wire

sharpshooter to take aim at a careless soldier. The space between opposing trenches was called no-man's-land.

A typical trench defense would have machine guns covering all the land approaching the defended trench, as well as some sort of barbed-wire system to slow the oncoming soldiers. A reasonably well defended trench could withstand an attack by a force many times its size. Attacks on a line of trenches would start with a horrible artillery bombardment, sometimes using poison gas such as mustard gas. The artillery attack would drive the defenders out of the exposed forward trenches and into the second line of trenches, which were deeper and more fortified. There would be deliberate lulls in the shelling, during which each force hoped to draw the other out into the open.

Over the top!

As the planned bombardment neared its end, the attacking troops would gather at their own front line and then, when the signal was given, come out of their trench, going over the top of the sandbags to make a dash for the enemy's trenches.

The result of these charges into the face of death was devastating. Both sides had a very high rate of men killed. The area between the trenches would be filled with human and animal bodies as well as the wounded. Men often lost their hearing as shell after shell burst around them. The ground shook from the impact. Perhaps there would be a dreaded gas attack, which would burn the skin and lungs. The Germans started using gas first, but other nations soon followed suit.

The standard defense against a gas attack was for each man to yell "Gas!" as loudly as he could. This would expel the air from his lungs and with it, hopefully, the first of the gas as he struggled to put on his gas mask before taking another breath of carbon-filtered air.

The war dragged on for months, and then years, becoming known as a war of attrition. Germany had the superior army but could not defeat the French and British on land. The German high command decided to try to use another high-tech weapon, the U-boat—submarine—to isolate Great Britain. Britain is an island nation, and the Germans planned to sink any ships bringing in vital supplies. The U-boats were spectacularly successful at first, but less so when the British used convoys, cargo ships accompanied by war vessels to protect them.

German submarine

By 1916 both Great Britain and France were suffering from the financial drain of the war, the human costs, and the loss of imports. It seemed to be a matter of who could last another year or so, or perhaps just a few more months. There was rationing of food and materials in England and France, and there were severe food shortages in Germany and Austria-Hungary.

The United States began to ship more and more food and supplies to Great Britain. President Wilson had promised that the United States would not enter the war, but America had become the major supporter of the Allied Powers. The Central Powers, led by Germany, needed to do something to offset the American aid. German submarines had already attacked some American cargo ships. Arthur Zimmermann, the German foreign secretary, sent a telegram to Mexican officials that was discovered by the British Navy and decoded. The communiqué is commonly referred to as the Zimmermann Telegram.

We intend to begin unrestricted submarine warfare on February 1. We shall nevertheless endeavor to keep America neutral. In the event that this does not succeed, we propose to Mexico an alliance on the following basis: Make war together, make peace together. Generous financial support, and approval on our part that Mexico recapture previously lost territory in Texas, New Mexico, and Arizona. The settlement details are left to Your Excellency.

Your Excellency will inform the President [of Mexico] of the above in utmost secrecy as soon as the outbreak of war with the United States of America is certain, and add the suggestion that he should, on his own initiative, invite Japan to join in immediately and at the same time mediate between ourselves and Japan. Please call the President's attention to the fact that the ruthless employment of our submarines now offers the prospect of compelling England to make peace within a few months.

The message had been sent on January 19, 1917. It reflected a sense of German desperation. Mexico could do very little in an attack against the United States, but Germany didn't have many options. American sentiment had already begun to turn in favor of the English. Americans still remembered the *Lusitania*, a British ship that had been sunk by the Germans in May of 1915, with the loss of 128 American lives. President Wilson knew that the Zimmerman Telegram signaled even more attacks and more American losses.

On April 2, 1917, President Woodrow Wilson gave a speech outlining the necessity of war with Germany. In it he stated that the world must be made safe for democracy. It was a momentous occasion for all Americans, many of whom felt that the war currently

President Woodrow Wilson

raging in Europe was too distant to be the business of the United States. Four days later, on April 6, Congress formally declared war on Germany.

THE PROBLEM OF RACE

lthough free since 1865, most African Americans lived under very poor conditions at the start of the war in Europe. Most lived in the South and worked on farms in rural areas. Southern agriculture—the cotton industry, tobacco, rice, and other crops— was dependent on inexpensive black labor. A number of factors severely limited the opportunities for the African American worker. The major limitation was segregation.

There were two kinds of segregation. One was segregation by law. In 1896 a Supreme Court decision, *Plessy v. Ferguson*, declared that companies, cities, towns, or states could separate people by race as long as the facilities for each race were "equal." Throughout the South and in many Northern areas as well, African Americans were forced to drink from "colored" fountains; go to "colored" schools, parks, and playgrounds; and even use special entrances to public places. The separate facilities were almost never "equal." Some Southern communities had no schools for black students and would hire teachers for only a few months per year to teach African Americans.

Besides the legal segregation there was an entrenched social segregation as well. Blacks were not hired for certain jobs, or given the same wages as whites. Blacks were not allowed to try on clothing in department stores and were often refused admittance to hotels and restaurants that elected to be "whites only."

The poll tax, a tax of one dollar or more for the privilege of voting, was established in some communities; this prevented blacks from voting and trying to change the laws. The social attitude in the Southern states was based on establishing the superiority of whites over blacks. Southerners did not want to treat blacks as equals and were not forced to by either laws or traditions.

There was racial prejudice in the North, too. Blacks were not allowed to buy houses or rent apartments in certain neighborhoods, and did not get certain jobs despite their qualifications. But the growing Northern industries, with their hunger for workers to manufacture the products they would sell around the world, offered far more than the Southern fields. Also, almost all Northern cities had either integrated schools or adequate schools in black neighborhoods. Northern children could learn to read and write. Black men in the North could vote. The Northern cities looked better and better to black families.

The years from 1913 to 1915 were particularly difficult for

Southern farmers. Boll weevils, a very hardy and destructive beetle, had infested Southern cotton fields to such an extent that many farmers, white and black, lost their entire crops. Floods in parts of Mississippi and Arkansas had also been disastrous. At the same time, Northern factories were turning out more and more products for the war in Europe and looking for workers. Large factories would send recruiters to the South to try to lure black men northward. Southern legislators, seeing the increased flow of black families from the South to the North, wondered what effect this migration would have on Southern agriculture and the South itself.

When the United States entered the war, there was another factor to consider. What would be the effect of African Americans' participation in the war? What would happen if black men left the farms in large numbers? How would their experiences in the military affect their acceptance of second-class citizenship in the South after the war? Would they come back to the segregated South and continue working in the fields, or would they look for other places to settle?

Some African Americans thought that the black man should not try to make the world "safe for democracy" until he had a fair share of that democracy in his own country. Others wanted a commitment from the United States that there would be an end to lynching, the

Black tenant farmers

Black tenant farmers were indispensable to the white South

terror tactic by which so many black men and women lost their lives through mob violence.

The National Association for the Advancement of Colored People (NAACP) sent letters to President Wilson asking him to speak up in favor of equal rights for all Americans. Southern legislators also approached the president with their concerns.

W.E.B. DuBois, editor of the NAACP's magazine *The Crisis* and an outspoken critic of domestic racial policies, was urging African Americans to participate in the war: "Let us, while this war lasts, forget our special grievances and close our ranks shoulder to shoulder with our white fellow citizens and the allied nations that are fighting for democracy."

Although the nation was officially at war, Southern politicians looked beyond the war and wondered how the military experience would affect race relations in the South. Southern Negroes had grown accustomed to the traditions of the region. Blacks knew that they had to be polite and respectful to whites while not expecting the same treatment for themselves. Black men were rarely called "mister" or "sir," no matter their position. Blacks who had lived in the North and were more likely to ask for equal treatment were considered troublemakers by Southerners.

President Wilson listened to the concerns of Southern legislators. They felt that if the racial balance was to be maintained in the South, special consideration would have to be given to the status of the black male as soldier. People who believed in racial superiority of

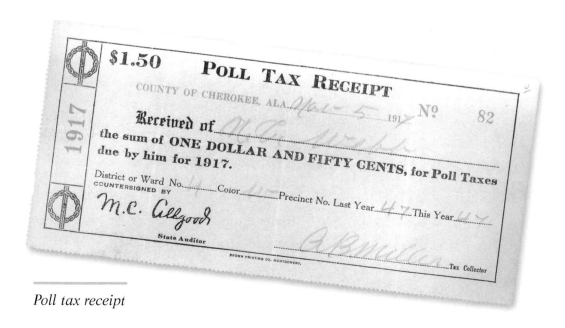

Poll tax receipt

"Economic Slavery": Political cartoon from Crisis *magazine*

whites did not want black men commanding whites, or even expecting equal treatment.

The nation was at war, but the racial conflict between blacks and whites was more important to some people than victory or defeat on the battlefield. President Wilson consulted his generals and both Northern and Southern politicians. Emmett J. Scott, an African American, was appointed as a special assistant to the secretary of war. Scott had been the assistant to Booker T. Washington, who endorsed the idea of segregation. Scott agreed in principle with Washington's feelings that blacks should accept the conditions given them by whites.

As the American military began to draw up its plans for war, the African American community knew that it would be facing many problems.

THE NATIONAL GUARD

Today, the United States is defended militarily by its armed forces. The Army, Navy, Air Force, Marine Corps, and Coast Guard are currently part of the United States' federal system. The training and deployment of these forces are determined by the president, who is the commander in chief; the president's staff; and the military commanders under the president. The National Guard is controlled jointly by the federal government and the state governments. In times of national emergencies the various National Guard units can be called into federal service. At these times they function no differently from regular army units.

When the United States was first formed, the state militias, as the units that would develop into the National Guard were called, differed from state to state. In most states all able-bodied men were considered part of the militia and received some training. There was both pride and security in the creation of these militias. The citizen-soldiers felt that they were protecting their own homes and land. They did so willingly and, for the most part, without pay. It was clear that in the slave states there would be no black people armed and trained to fight. But in the free states there was also a problem. Military personnel have ranks that are independent of social issues. There are two categories of rank: noncommissioned personnel and commissioned officers. The noncommissioned personnel ranks range from private to sergeant major. Each individual of a particular rank is the equal to others of that rank and above those in a lower rank.

Commissioned officers have a special status and are accorded special respect in the services. Enlisted men (noncommissioned) are obliged to salute all officers encountered in public and to come to attention when an officer enters a room unless given other instructions.

In the case of both noncommissioned personnel and commissioned officers, the rank of the soldier is the primary factor determining authority. Commissioned officers were to be saluted and addressed as "sir." This meant that black officers would have to be treated with a courtesy that was routinely denied them in civilian life. Many white resented this forced recognition. The way to avoid conflicts was to simply not include blacks in the state militias.

New York state had one of the nation's largest militias, consisting of a number of regiments. In 1824 New York's 7th Regiment began calling itself the "National Guard" after the Garde National of France, which was headed by the Marquis de Lafayette, who had aided America so much during the Revolutionary War. Soon other state militias began calling themselves the National Guard.

At the outbreak of the Civil War many National Guard units were called into federal service. When more men were needed, both sides—the Union army and the Confederate army—accepted enlistees and also had forced service—the draft.

The war began with only white soldiers in actual combat roles, and with blacks performing as laborers in both armies. But eventually blacks were allowed to fight in the Union army, and more than 180,000 men served in it.

By the outbreak of the Spanish-American War in April 1898, there were several black National Guard units, the best established being the 8th Illinois Infantry. The war lasted scarcely four months, from April to August 1898. Many black units, including the 8th Illinois and the 24th Infantry, participated in this war, which greatly reduced Spanish influence in the Americas.

In 1908 Congress passed laws stating that if National Guard units were

Officer, 8th Illinois Infantry   called to federal service, they would enter as complete units instead of simply supplying men to be assigned according to the needs of the government.

The federal government also dictated the size and composition of the state National Guards and the levels of fitness and training required for national recognition. The formation of the state National Guard units could be initiated by the governor of a state or by an individual. By 1910 the black press in New York often carried articles suggesting that a black (or "colored") National Guard unit be formed in New York that would be the equal of the 8th Illinois in Chicago. The 8th Illinois, with its black officers, was an effective fighting unit and also a demonstration of the capabilities of black men in leadership positions.

Charles W. Fillmore, a handsome, politically astute man, had been a first lieutenant in the 9th U.S. Volunteer Infantry, which served with distinction in the Spanish-American War. After the war he got involved in Ohio politics. He became a confidant of George A. Myers, a black politician who also ran a nationally famous barbershop. Myers had a reputation as a power broker and aided Republicans throughout the state in obtaining black votes. Seeing how Myers maneuvered his way through the seats of power in Ohio, Fillmore understood that the path to the creation of a black regiment in New York would depend largely on what political power he could achieve. If he could assemble a regiment and somehow bring it up to the needed manpower, the legislature would have to authorize its official state recognition. Then, if the legislature provided funding, he would need the governor's back-

COLORED MEN WANTED

Between the ages of 18 and 45 years

FOR

Colored Regiment

NOW ORGANIZING

We want a Regiment in the State National Guard

We want an Armory and everything that goes with a Regiment

We CAN get it by intelligent organization

Would you like to see a Regiment in the State of New York with Colored Officers?

Would you like to see that Regiment quartered in a fine Armory?

IF SO

ENROLL YOUR NAME TODAY

Six hundred men have already enlisted and all vacancies will soon be filled

APPLY AT ONCE

TO THE HEADQUARTERS OF THE

FIRST COLORED PROVISIONAL REGIMENT OF INFANTRY

343 W. 40th St., New York (TOP FLOOR FRONT)

RECRUITING OFFICERS

Captain R. S. DAVIS

Lieut. A. M. ALSTON   Lieut. J. CORKSON

Colonel CHAS. W. FILLMORE, Commanding

Captain J. ALBERT JAXON, Adjutant

T. IAS PRESS, 117 West 30th Street New York

Charles W. Fillmore tried to raise a black regiment

ing to have the appropriate legislation enacted. Supported by the black press, he began a campaign for an all-black regiment. He planned to personally select its officers and lead the regiment as colonel.

Fillmore began recruiting in New York City and upstate New York, making direct appeals at public meetings, advertising in the newspapers, and posting bulletins throughout the state. He also accepted applications from nearby states, such as New Jersey and Pennsylvania. As the number of enrollees grew, Fillmore began to put them through their paces, teaching fundamental marching skills in parks and parade fields around New York.

African Americans were gaining power in New York City simply by dint of their numbers. New York politicians began supporting, at least in public, the idea of a black regiment. The state legislature passed two bills authorizing the governor to establish such a unit. The first was not signed by the governor, and nothing came of the effort. The second was signed by Governor William Sulzer in June 1913. Fillmore was, at first, elated. But Sulzer left office a few months after the bill was signed, without establishing the regiment. Fillmore, nearing fifty years of age, saw his dream fading.

6

THE FIGHTING 15TH

In 1916 the New York National Guard was activated to fight along the Mexican border against Pancho Villa, a hero of the Mexican Revolution. Villa had fought bravely and well against a brutal Mexican dictator but later fell out with his fellow revolutionary Venustiano Carranza. When the United States officially recognized Carranza as president of Mexico, Villa began a series of raids along the Mexican border. The United States activated the New York National Guard, and soon the troops were on their way south. So many New York troops were being used in Mexico or being called up for the war in Europe that a need for a new regiment became apparent.

Governor Charles S. Whitman, who had become governor of New York in 1914, asked William Hayward, a personal friend, to recruit and form the regiment that would be called the 15th New

York National Guard, or the 15th Infantry Regiment, ignoring Fillmore's earlier efforts. Hayward, who was white, was then serving as the public service commissioner. It was understood that if the regiment was successfully formed, Hayward would become its colonel instead of Fillmore. Fillmore was offered and accepted a position as a captain.

The black press and public knew that this would probably mean that most of the officers in the unit would be white. There was sufficient precedent for this belief. In the regular army units superior officers, even those commanding predominantly black units, were all white. There were many complaints within the African American community, but there were many supporters of the proposed regiment as well.

Black leaders understood the conflict in Europe and fully recognized America's growing involvement. They knew that if America did enter the war, the most advantageous position for African Americans would be to join the national army as complete units of the National Guard. National Guard units had their own officers, as well as their own opportunities for advancement within their units. Black Americans were aware of what the black National Guard unit in Illinois, the 8th Illinois, had accomplished.

The actual formation of the 15th did not begin until mid-June 1916. By then the war in Europe had already claimed thousands of lives, and the possibility of the United States entering the conflict became a probability. Colonel Hayward began putting together a core group of men, black and white, to help in the recruitment process. He would call on businessmen, entertainers, teachers, architects, and New York's upper class to create the outstanding regiment he hoped for.

The original armory building was the basement of the Lafayette Theater, a Harlem landmark that had seen productions of Shakespeare as well as performances by blues and jazz singers. The Lafayette reflected Harlem's growing importance as a vibrant black community. The area from 125th Street northward to 145th on the west side of Manahattan was the heart of Harlem. Black families moved into the area from other New York City neighborhoods

Harlem had its own canteen for black soldiers

but also, in increasing numbers, from the Southern states.

The first guardsmen of the 15th were from all around New York state, with the majority coming from Manhattan and Brooklyn. While the officers of the regiment could officially be either white or black, the rank and file would all be black. Hayward decided to recruit from the top down and worked hard to attract the best officers he could find. He knew of Fillmore's disappointment at not heading the 15th but still felt that he wanted the top positions to be filled by whites. Hayward used Fillmore to convince black professionals to join the 15th and to carry the message to young men from the black areas of the state that a colored regiment would be a source of pride for all of them.

Hayward's first task was to fulfill the federal regulations for a National Guard unit, so that the state could apply for supplies and funding from the national government. He hounded shooting clubs and other National Guard units for surplus weapons and uniforms and sought donations from New York's elite society. A major coup was attracting Hamilton Fish Jr. to the organization. Ham Fish, as he was known, was a wealthy and influential socialite. One of his ancestors had been governor of New York. Fish was also on good terms with one of the most successful black men in America, James Reese Europe.

Europe was a well-known composer and musician. His orchestra had provided the music for the internationally popular white dance team of Irene and Vernon Castle. When Europe was approached by

Candidates for officer training

Hayward to join the 15th, he was hesitant. He had been interested earlier, when he thought the 15th would be commanded solely by black officers, which would have been a major boost for the officers involved and for African Americans in general. But in 1916, already a star in the musical world, he was more interested in continuing his career on Broadway. What's more, he had already transcended the color line, orchestrating and composing for entertainers of all races.

Hayward changed his approach to Europe. Since both black and white leaders thought that a colored National Guard unit was a worthwhile project, Europe would be doing a service to his race by joining it and adding his name to the luster of the adventure. Hayward also said that he would try to get Europe the kind of band that would make the New York community proud.

Europe believed in the fraternity of black men. He had organized groups of black musicians and belonged to a number of black social organizations. After giving the matter a lot of thought, Europe decided that he would join on condition that he could put together an orchestra that would be considerably larger than the traditional military band. He also wanted to select his own musicians. This was a difficult task under military regulations, but Hayward felt that James Reese Europe might well be the most important person he would recruit. Hayward approached New York's upper-class patrons of the theater arts and was soon able to raise the money for Europe's expanded orchestra.

What Europe wanted to do was to create a national Negro orchestra that would rival any in the world. He saw the formation of a band for the 15th as the beginning of such an organization. He agreed to join the 15th and to convince his friend and fellow musician Noble Sissle to join as well.

With Europe's name attached to the regiment, other notable blacks, as well as many ordinary citizens, joined. By April 8, 1917, the regiment had reached its peacetime size of 1,378 men. This fulfilled the federal standard for size, and the 15th was given its own flag, or "colors." The unit, now with federal recognition and additional funding, was then given authorization to recruit more men, bringing it up to nearly two thousand volunteers, the strength of a wartime unit.

A wide range of men had joined the 15th New York National Guard. The joining of prominent men was reported by the black press, and the 15th soon became a source of pride within the African American community. For already successful men such as Europe and Fillmore, the 15th was an opportunity to show the world, and their own community, what talented black men could achieve. For others, some who had had few individual successes, the 15th was a chance to be with successful people and to accomplish goals as a team. It also meant a chance to work and live in a situation in which equality was measured by rank, not skin color.

Patriotism was also an important consideration for the men joining the 15th. The United States was their country, and its battles were their battles. Black Americans enrolled eagerly, proud to wear the uniform and proud to take up arms in the cause of preserving democracy.

The problems of mistreatment and abuse of African Americans, however, were clear, and W.E.B. DuBois addressed them in *The Crisis*. Recognizing that African Americans were still being lynched and segregated, and denied educational opportunities and, in many places, voting rights, he nevertheless urged black Americans to put aside their differences for the duration of the war and to take up America's struggle.

❦ EDITORIAL ❦

This is the crisis of the world. For all the long years to come men will point to the year 1918 as the great Day of Decision, the day when the world decided whether it would submit to military despotism and an endless armed peace if peace it could be called or whether they would put down the menace of German militarism and inaugurate the United States of the World.

We of the colored race have no ordinary interest in the outcome. That which the German power represents today spells death to the aspirations of Negroes and all darker races for equality, freedom and democracy. Let us not hesitate. We make no ordinary sacrifice, but we make it gladly and willingly with our eyes lifted to the hills. Let us, while this war lasts, forget our special grievances and close our ranks shoulder to shoulder with our own white fellow citizens and the allied nations that are fighting for democracy.

W.E.B. DuBois
The Crisis, July 1918

Left: Black recruits

Right: 15th National Guard color bearers

Below: Black volunteers show the flag

WHO WOULD LEAD COLORED MEN INTO BATTLE?

Even as the black regiment was being formed in New York, the debate as to the role of African Americans in the army was being argued. The country was in a war mode. American flags and banners hung from windows. Recruiting posters appeared with proud images of young white Americans standing up for their country. But the enlistments—those men volunteering to enter the armed forces—would not be enough to put an army into the field. The sheer numbers of men needed to engage in the war suggested that eventually the United States would have to bring men into military service on a nonvoluntary basis, and plans were drawn to do so. Such a draft would involve a wide range of men, black and white.

While the laws governing the National Guard said that the individual regiments, battalions, etc., would enter federal service as whole units, men who were called up by the draft would be placed wherever

Official Government Notice

EVERY MAN

Between the ages of 18 to 45 (both inclusive), except those previously registered

MUST REGISTER

for the

Selective Service Draft

Exact date of registration to be announced by Official Proclamation. Be ready, find out when to register, and where to register. Registration will take place early in

SEPTEMBER

Penalty for Failure to Register

is one year imprisonment, and NO man can exonerate himself by the payment of a fine.

Register Promptly!

E. H. CROWDER
Provost Marshal General
War Department, U. S. A.

(Read Other Side Carefully)

Draft flyer

the military needed them. People in the black community felt that no blacks would be called into the service as officers. A proposal was made by Joel E. Spingarn to open a school for black officers.

The fact that the school would be exclusively for black officers was not easily accepted in the African American community. It was, to many, volunteer segregation. But Spingarn, a white man from a prominent family long interested in seeking equality for blacks, saw the issue differently.

MILITARY TRAINING CAMP FOR COLORED MEN

An Open Letter from Dr. J. E. Spingarn

New York, February 15, 1917.

To the Educated Colored Men of the United States:

It is of the highest importance that the educated colored men of this country should be given opportunities for leadership. You must cease to remain in the background in every field of national activity, and must come forward to assume your right places as leaders of American life. All of you cannot be leaders, but those of you who have the capacity for leadership must be given an opportunity to test and display it.

There is now just such an opportunity possible for you, in case of war, to become leaders and officers instead of followers and privates. **Major General Leonard Wood,** of the

U.S. Army, commanding the Department of the East, **has promised that if two hundred of you apply for admission, he will organize and maintain a military training camp for colored men, with just the sort of training to fit you to serve as officers of volunteers in case of war.**

I do not believe that colored men should be separated from other Americans in any field of life; but the crisis is too near at hand to discuss principles and opinions, and it seems to me that there is only one thing for you to do at this juncture, and that is to get the training that will fit you to be officers, however and wherever and whenever this training may be obtained. **If two hundred of you do not send applications immediately, the opportunity may be lost forever.**

The camp will be conducted on exactly the same principles as the military training camp held at Plattsburgh, N.Y., where thousands of men have received intensive training in military service. It will be under the direction of United States Army officers. It will last **four weeks.** The date has not been fixed, but it will probably begin **early in June.** The status of every student at the camp will be that of a cadet, just as at West Point.

I understand that the transportation to and from the camp will be defrayed by the government, and that the subsistence and training at the camp will be free. It is probable that every man will have to pay his own fare to the camp, and that after he arrives, his travelling expenses will be refunded, and his fare home paid. The only expense will be the cost of the uniform, which each man must furnish himself. This consists of a khaki blouse, khaki breeches, two olive drab shirts, web belt, campaign hat and cotton leggings, costing in all about eight or ten dollars. Any good russet walking shoes will do. The outfit may be purchased on arrival at camp, or better still, from the Army and Navy Co-operative Company, with branches in New York, Washington and Philadelphia. Almost any sporting goods store can furnish the outfit, which must be of the regular army pattern. Those who wish to do some study in advance are advised to read Moss's Manual of Military Training.

Candidates must be between the ages of 20 and 45, in vigorous health, and of good moral character. Men who are graduates or undergraduates of colleges, high-schools, normal, agricultural, or industrial schools, or other institutions of learning, are preferred; but any man of intelligence, character, and ability may join. Previous military experience is not necessary. If you are not a graduate or undergraduate of some institution, it might be advisable to have a letter of recommendation from some person of repute. . . .

Sincerely yours,

J. E. SPINGARN

One of the first black men who applied to the officer training school was James E. Gould.

African Americans had been enlisting in the United States Navy long before they were officially accepted into the Army. When the U.S.S. *Niagara* slid into blockade position during the Civil War, she had a number of black sailors, among whom was William B. Gould. For Gould, joining the Union forces was a chance to both preserve the Union and strike a blow against slavery. It was a chance that he could not let go by.

More than fifty years later Gould was still talking about his part in the combat in service to his country. On May 30, 1917, the veterans known as members of the Grand Army of the Republic met in Dedham, Massachusetts, to honor the members of the Union army who had been killed during the Civil War and to discuss the present war raging in Europe.

James E. Gould, William's son, listened attentively as the older men spoke of past glories. The army was drafting African Americans to fight in the war, and young James wanted to be part of the effort to make the world safe for democracy. He had already applied to the officer training school in Plattsburgh, New York, only to be told that his application was "on hold" until the War Department decided what it would do with colored soldiers.

What was not acceptable, to James or to other African Americans talking about the war, was the practice of creating

James E. Gould
1st. Lieut. 357th Inf.

NUMBER 53
OCCASIONAL PAPERS
ENGINEER SCHOOL
UNITED STATES ARMY

Lessons in Fortification

PART I
Effects of Artillery Fire

PART II
Field Fortification and the Protection of Batteries

WASHINGTON BARRACKS, D. C.
PRESS OF THE ENGINEER SCHOOL
1917

Above: James Gould's graduating class in Iowa

Left: Army training manual

outfits consisting of black enlisted men and white officers. When the Plattsburgh school refused black applicants, a group of local citizens decided to create a school for colored officers. The Architectural School of Military Engineering (Colored) was established in Boston, and Gould attended it.

There was also a push to create a special school for African American officers in Des Moines, Iowa. The idea of a segregated facility met with considerable resistance. Black men were being asked to risk their lives to

preserve democracy, yet they were being segregated in their own homeland. Nevertheless, James and his brother Herbert applied to the school. All six of the Gould brothers were either in the military or in the process of trying to enlist. But after the GAR meeting James decided that he did not want to wait until the War Department made up its mind. On May 31, 1917, the day after the GAR meeting, James E. Gould enlisted in the United States Army at Fort Banks, in Massachusetts. His diary reads:

> *Here the doctors went over me carefully examining*
> *eyes, teeth, heart, lungs, etc. All went well till I stepped*
> *on the scales to be weighed.*
>
> *The scales had the needle set for 120 pounds,*
> *the minimum weight to be accepted in the army, and*
> *to my surprise the needle refused to budge. Then, when*
> *the soldier assisting the doctor moved the balance,*
> *I who called my weight about 120–125 pounds, found*
> *that in Nature's garb I weighed just 115 pounds.*

Gould was, nevertheless, accepted into the army with the warning that he would have to gain the needed weight. A few days later he was notified that he had been accepted into the Officer Candidate School in Iowa.

Headquarters Northeastern Department

Boston, Massachusetts

June 5, 1917

. . . 12. Each of the following-named colored citizens of New England, having been recommended under the provisions of Memoranduym [sic], these hedquarters [sic], dated May 24, 1917, is authorized to report to the Camp Commander, Ft. Des Moisnes [sic], Ia., on June 15 1917, for training.

James Edward Gould, 303 Milton St., Dedham

Army order

Gould arrived at the camp on the assigned date and started the arduous training. He enjoyed the rigors of the physical workouts and the discipline. Here he was taught a full range of military subjects, which he handled with ease. He also saw many of the candidates fail the difficult course and came to realize that the army was still not sure that it wanted African American officers. Gould wrote in his diary:

All went well till at the end of the first month's training when we were ordered once more to be examined. Of course I had no means of knowing whether I had gained or lost weight from the extensive training. So before time to march to the gym I drank all of the water I could hold and when I stepped on the scale the needle went up to 122 pounds. It was a great and glorious feeling as at this examination a number of candidates were dismissed from camp for various physical defects.

The entire camp was under the command of Colonel Charles C. Ballou, a Southerner whose attitude toward blacks was rooted in the region and practices from which he had come. There were incidents of overt racism around Des Moines and nearby areas. Colonel Ballou's reaction was to warn the young black men that they were not to make trouble. By the end of the training many of the would-be officers were discouraged and ready to go home. Colonel Ballou was promoted to major general.

Charles C. Ballou

As the training neared an end, there were rumors that the War Department was still not sure what it would do with the black officers.

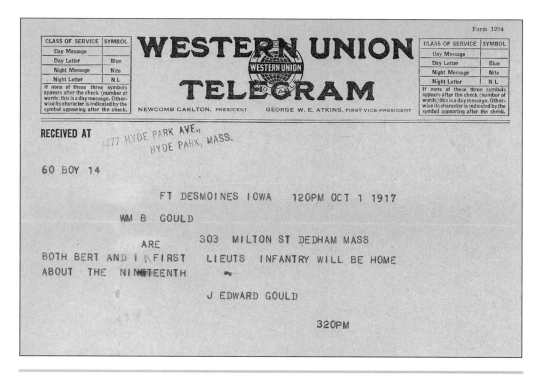

Gould has successfully completed training

But on Wednesday, October 10, 1917, the training was over and the men who had mastered the academics and physical rigors of officer training finally received their commissions. James E. Gould, barely 120 pounds, was a first lieutenant in the United States Army.

Joel E. Spingarn had not been happy with the segregated school, but he knew that any school would either be segregated or not exist at all. He believed that no matter how they began, the young officers would eventually prove themselves on the field of battle.

TRAINING THE BLACK SOLDIER

P roper training is essential to the military experience. It is by training that individual soldiers learn to function as a fighting unit. The men of the 15th—laborers, clerks, lawyers, artists, salesmen—all had to understand how an infantry unit fought and their own roles within the unit. They also had to develop confidence in the abilities of their officers and their fellow soldiers. In turn the officers had to understand and appreciate just what their men could and would do under trying circumstances. A successful bond between officers and enlisted men, framed in mutual respect, invariably results in fewer casualties in combat. It is during training that the bond begins.

There were already stories circulating around the country of black men getting inferior training from white officers. In some

WAR DEPARTMENT

OFFICE OF THE CHIEF OF STAFF,

War Plans Division, Washington. E. & R. Branch.

LITERACY TEST.

(C)

OBJECT OF TEST.—This test measures literacy insofar as it demands a power to read and follow simple instructions, an elementary ability to figure, and a little common information.

DIRECTIONS FOR GIVING TEST.—See that the man is furnished with a sharp pencil. Hand out the blank and say clearly, " Do what it tells you to do. Answer all the questions you can." You may repeat these directions but you must give no other help whatsoever. If the man does not understand what he has to do, or asks for your aid, merely repeat to him, " Do what it tells you to do. Answer all the questions you can." Allow the man as long as he needs. At the close of the examination be sure and see that the name is clearly written.

SCORING THE TEST.—One point is given for each correct answer or element, making a total of twenty on the test. The test may be destroyed after scores have been determined and made of record in the organization.

3—7679

Form E. & R. 100c

Above: Recruits

Left: Literacy test for black applicants

camps the white soldiers lived in barracks while the blacks had to sleep outdoors. At Camp Meade, Maryland, some white soldiers made a film parodying the black men they were supposed to be training. When there were uniform shortages, it was the black soldiers who did without. Some training units were given old Civil War uniforms in which to train. Literacy tests were used to justify assigning blacks to labor units.

The 15th had been officially recognized by the federal government, and Colonel Hayward, the white commander, worked hard to equip his men, often using private funds and facilities. The black companies under his command deserved respect from the white officers over them, but they also had to balance that respect with discipline and a willingness to make the sacrifices needed to be soldiers.

The instant respect that James Europe's band achieved, and its praise in white newspapers, went a long way toward creating the sense of unit pride that Hayward had hoped for. The music that Europe played, a combination of pop, ragtime, jazz, and military marches, was largely familiar to the soldiers.

The officers of the 15th had all volunteered to serve with the black outfit. Many were men from wealthy families and had attended elite schools. More important, their attitude toward the soldiers they commanded was excellent. They expected a high level of performance from their men and were not hesitant to demand it. They knew that the black outfits would be looked upon as social experiments as well as military units. Black soldiers from the 54th Massachusetts had demonstrated their mettle during the Civil War and had proven that black men were as brave as any. Bravery, however, was not enough against a well-trained army.

The highest-ranking black officers were Napoleon B. Marshall, a graduate of Harvard, and Charles W. Fillmore. They were both captains. Besides being exceptionally bright, Marshall was a nationally known athlete. Fillmore had years of military experience. Benjamin Robeson, from Princeton, New Jersey, joined the unit as one of three chaplains.

Many of the officers were young, barely out of college, while others, such as Fillmore and Captain Arthur W. Little, were men in the twilight of their military careers. Little was already forty-three, old for a company commander, but he was a dedicated soldier and New Yorker who respected the men he led.

The regiment did not have its own facilities, and so the various battalions often trained in different areas of the country. They even trained in New York City's parks, as did other National Guard units.

An infantry *regiment* is a military unit consisting of at least 1,500 men. Each regiment has two or more *battalions*, each consisting of at least 700 men. The battalion, in turn, is made up of four or more *companies*, each made up of 175 men. The companies are made up of *platoons* of 40 or so men. A platoon is made up of nine- or ten-man *squads*. Each of these military units has responsibilities within its own unit and within the overall regiment.

The 15th, like all military units, first went about learning the complex commands of marching and close-order drill. Marching in lines sometimes twelve men wide demanded concentration and timing and instilled the notion that the unit was working together. They were issued rifles and machine guns and taught to maintain them and fire at targets. Each man had to attain a proficiency in taking a weapon apart while blindfolded and reassembling it. They also had to keep the weapons perfectly clean to avoid malfunctions. In Peekskill, New York, part of the regiment took several weeks of training in May 1917, the month after President Wilson had declared war against Germany.

Right: Recruits at Lexington, Kentucky

Below: Basic training

Above: Basic education

The papers were filled with news of the war, and much of the conversation among the men was about its mounting human costs. Estimates of French and British losses were staggering. Never before had such terrible weapons been used. Men in trenches were being gassed. They were being burned out of their holes with flamethrowers. Machine guns cut down charging soldiers by the hundreds.

The 15th broke camp at Peekskill on May 30 and boarded a train for New York City, where they joined other National Guard units to march up Riverside Drive. Captain Arthur Little thought that the men's training was good in close-order drill but not adequate in combat infantry training. He felt that would come later. By the time they left Peekskill, the men had learned to conduct themselves like soldiers, to keep their equipment clean, and to accept military discipline. It was a good first step.

In July the 15th was officially called up and mustered into the United States Army. They would eventually become part of the 93rd Division (Provisional).

The War Department had decided to create two colored divisions, the 92nd and the 93rd. An army division is made up of a number of units that, together, can be used to fulfill a predetermined military assignment. The divisions were designed to have combat regiments to do the actual fighting and other units, such as supply, medical, and engineers, to support the fighting troops. The 93rd did not have all the components of a full division and was therefore listed as provisional.

Their first assignment under federal jurisdiction, while still flying the colors of the 15th, was guard duty throughout New York State.

In 1917 there were thousands of German Americans living in the United States. There were also many people who sympathized with the German cause. There were concerns that any of these might try to sabotage American interests. The 15th was used to guard some possible targets. A battalion was sent to Yaphank, on Long Island, where German sympathizers met on a regular basis. Another company was sent to Ellis Island to guard German prisoners. A small group of soldiers was sent to the Brooklyn Navy Yard.

But even as the 15th was doing its part to protect the United States, violence against blacks continued throughout the country. Lynch mobs terrorized black communities, and segregation seemed to be growing stronger. Black soldiers found themselves in a dilemma. On the one hand they were being trained to risk their lives in defense of the country, while on the other hand they were being told to accept their role as inferior citizens.

In New York the NAACP staged protests against the violence. Referring to President Woodrow Wilson's speech claiming that American participation in the war would make the world safe for democracy, signs asked President Wilson when he would make America safe for democracy.

The black press throughout the country began to extol the patriotism, dedication, and pride of the black soldier. When famous African Americans such as James Reese Europe enlisted, it was often

reported in the white press as well. Northern factories began to send representatives to Southern cities recruiting black workers. Southern legislators began to press President Wilson for a definite plan to minimize the effect of military service on black soldiers. They wanted the relationship between whites and blacks, especially in the South, to remain the same as it had been before the war.

In response, Newton D. Baker, the secretary of war, who was from Martinsburg, West Virginia, appointed a black man from the Tuskegee Institute, Emmett J. Scott, to be a special assistant to the War Department as an advisor on black affairs. Scott had been an

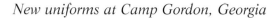
New uniforms at Camp Gordon, Georgia

assistant to Booker T. Washington in Alabama. Washington, who had died in 1915, had been known as a black leader willing to accept segregation and second-class citizenship for blacks in return for white support of his training programs. Scott's appointment as a special advisor to the War Department was not looked on favorably by blacks who hoped that African Americans would eventually benefit by their service to America during the war. Scott's mission was not only to discourage blacks from leaving the South but also to investigate protests among black soldiers. Southern communities took a more direct approach to keep the blacks in their midst from being influenced by Northerners.

SPARTANBURG, SOUTH CAROLINA

he summer of 1917 was hot and muggy. The cramped Harlem tenements were nearly unbearable at nights, and many Harlem residents slept on rooftops and fire escapes to catch whatever breezes were available. But when the 15th New York National Guard (Colored) was assigned for training at Camp Wadsworth in South Carolina, things promised to get even hotter.

The move had been anticipated and announced, and an article in *The New York Times* on August 31 had foretold of trouble.

Camp Wadsworth, Spartanburg, S.C., Aug. 30, 1917

Following the receipt of a report that the Government intended to alter its original plan and include the Fifteenth Infantry, colored, in the troops to be trained at the camp here, the City of Spartanburg officially protested to the War Department against the sending of these troops, on the ground that trouble might result if the Fifteenth refused to accept the limited liberties accorded to the city s colored population. Mayor J. F. Floyd, in his protest, called attention to the recent outbreak of negro troops at Houston, Texas.

That Colonel William B. Hayward s organization, one of the first of the city s regiments to reach its war strength, is unwelcome here is evident from the comments heard in the streets. The whites here are outspoken in their opposition to the plan and predict trouble if the War Department fails to heed the protest.

l was sorry to learn that the Fifteenth Regiment has been ordered here, said Mayor Floyd to-night, for, with their Northern ideas about race equality, they will probably expect to be treated like white men. I can say right here that they will not be treated as anything except negroes. We shall treat them exactly as we treat our resident negroes. This thing is like waving a red flag in the face of a bull, something that can t be done without trouble. We have asked Congressman Nicholls to request the War Department not to send the soldiers here. You remember the trouble a couple of weeks ago at Houston.

The "trouble" at Houston occurred when black soldiers of the 24th Infantry, stationed near Houston, reacted to what they felt had been white harassment by riding into town with their weapons. When they were met by a group of whites, there was an exchange of gunfire, and two blacks and seventeen whites were killed. Thirteen of the men who participated in what was officially labeled a "mutiny" were sentenced to be hanged.

While the sentiment against the 15th extended through all classes in the city, the opposition took form through the Chamber of Commerce, which put the matter before the Mayor.

Chamber of Commerce Objects

We asked for the camp for Spartanburg, said an official of the Chamber this afternoon, but at that time we understood that no colored troops were to be sent down. It is a great mistake to send Northern negroes down here, for they do not understand our attitude. We wouldn t mind it if the Government sent us a regiment of Southern negroes; we understand them and they understand us. But with those Northern fellows it s different.

I can tell you for certain that if any of those colored soldiers go in any of our soda stores and the like and ask to be served they ll be knocked down. Somebody will

> throw a bottle. We don t allow negroes to use the same glass that a white man may later have to drink out of. We have our customs down here, and we aren t going to alter them.

With the Houston mutiny still front-page material, and the *Times* article in mind, the 15th boarded trains for South Carolina.

Spartanburg, South Carolina, was basically a small agricultural community that had been settled shortly after the Revolutionary War. It had a "comfortable" relationship with its black population, meaning that the black population understood that the whites were the superior race and that they were not to make trouble by demanding such things as social equality, entrance to white establishments, or anything else that might make a white person feel uncomfortable. The problem of having black soldiers—black men with guns who were being trained to defend themselves against anyone designated as an enemy—was clear.

There was no doubt as to what could be expected from the Army if there was trouble. Major General Charles C. Ballou had made that clear in his widely circulated "Bulletin No. 35." Directed to the soldiers of the 92nd Division, also comprised of black soldiers, it was a reaction to the attempt by an African American sergeant to enter a theater in Kansas. There was no official policy in Kansas of segregation, but the owner refused to allow the soldier to enter.

The bulletin read:

Headquarters, 92nd Division

Camp Funston, Kans., March 28, 1918

1. It should be well known to all colored officers and men that no useful purpose is served by such acts as will cause the "color question" to be raised. It is not a question of legal rights, but a question of policy, and any policy that tends to bring about a conflict of races, with its resulting animosities, is prejudicial to the military interest of the 92nd Division, and therefore prejudicial to an important interest of the colored race.

2. To avoid such conflicts the Division Commander has repeatedly urged that all colored members of his command, and especially the officers and non-commissioned officers, should refrain from going where their presence will be resented. In spite of this injunction, one of the sergeants of the Medical Department has recently precipitated the precise trouble that should be avoided, and then called on the Division Commander to take sides in a row that should never have occurred had the sergeant placed the general good above his personal pleasure and convenience. The sergeant entered a theater, as he undoubtedly had a legal right to do, and precipitated trouble by making it possible to allege race

discrimination in the seat he was given. He is strictly within his legal rights in this matter, and the theater manager was legally wrong. Nevertheless the sergeant is guilty of the GREATER wrong in doing ANYTHING, NO MATTER HOW LEGALLY CORRECT, that will provoke race animosity.

3. The Division Commander repeats that the success of the Division with all that success implies, is dependent upon the good will of the public. That public is nine tenths white. White men made the Division, and they can break it just as easily if it becomes a trouble maker.

4. All concerned are again enjoined to place the general interest of the Division above personal pride and gratification. Avoid every situation that can give rise to racial ill-will. Attend quietly and faithfully to your duties, and don't go where your presence is not desired.

5. This will be read to all organizations of the 92nd Division.

By command of Major-General Ballou.

General Ballou's message was loud and clear. It didn't matter to him if what was happening to his men was legal or illegal. If there were local bigots who didn't want blacks around, then the blacks should stay away.

It was essential for soldiers to overcome their fears. The safety and well-being of the soldier, his regiment, and perhaps even

his country would depend on it. But for some Americans the idea of racial superiority had become the more important issue.

General Ballou, born in the South and raised in the traditions he was upholding, stated that white men had created the 15th and white men could break it up if it became a "trouble maker." But could the United States simply reject all black soldiers? What would the effect on the country have been? Rejected from the army, would blacks support the war effort? Would white soldiers fight if their black neighbors did not have to? It was an issue that threatened to tear the nation apart.

Many of the other white military units on the base defended the black soldiers, refusing to join in with the local racists. Northern

white soldiers often refused to patronize white stores that refused to serve black soldiers. Fights broke out between Northern and Southern units.

Spartanburg had asked for the military camp, knowing that it would be an economic boon for the area. But cheap black labor, which was abundant in South Carolina, was also an economic boon, one the South did not want to give up.

Emmett Scott was sent to Spartanburg to calm things down. He was not well received.

Scott's views concerning race relations matched those of his former boss, Booker T. Washington. Scott was anxious to please Secretary Baker and tried to ease the problem by speaking to the senior black enlisted men. His idea was that they should avoid racial trouble at all costs, and that their ability to get along with whites, no matter how personally disagreeable, would help the black cause.

Considerations of race clearly outweighed the needs of the country in Spartanburg in the fall of 1917. The problem for the small Southern city was that the inhabitants knew the war would not last forever, but their relationships with the black community would.

Not all of Spartanburg's residents went along with the mayor. Some invited Hayward and other white officers to sit down and talk about ways of avoiding trouble. A dance was arranged for the men, and the black citizens of Spartanburg invited the soldiers into their churches, into their homes, and into their hearts. The 15th's band, led by James Reese Europe and drum major Noble Sissle, played in the town square. It was probably the best music the town had ever heard, played by musicians whose fame would soon be worldwide.

But some residents of the small town were determined to make trouble. There was talk that black soldiers had insulted a white woman. There were several incidents in which black officers were abused by local toughs. But the most dangerous incident occurred when a rumor started that two black soldiers either had been or were about to be lynched. The talk quickly circulated through the regiment. A group of forty-three soldiers—men who had been trained to use their weapons and use them well—assembled and marched into town. Two soldiers went into the police station to inquire about the "missing men," while the others, their guns fully loaded, waited outside.

A black sergeant found out about the foray and reported it to Colonel Hayward. Hayward grabbed a vehicle and rushed into town, where he found the men waiting. He went into the police station, ascertained that the two men had never been in police custody, and hustled his soldiers out of town as quickly as he could.

Another serious incident occurred when Sergeant Noble Sissle and Lieutenant James Reese Europe encountered trouble in town. Noble Sissle was one of the most sophisticated and accomplished men in the 15th. A handsome, well-spoken man, he had directed a band; he wrote music, sang, and played for New York's high society. His manners were impeccable and his speech was perfect, making him just the kind of African American who annoyed bigots. Sissle had gone into a hotel lobby to buy a newspaper and was physically abused by a hotel employee. He made his way out onto the street, and a group of white soldiers took up his cause and threatened to tear up the hotel lobby, but they were stopped by James Reese Europe.

For the men of the 15th, and for the white soldiers who supported them, the incident emphasized the entire racial problem. Any white person intent on making trouble could undo all the goodwill that had been created, and the black soldiers could not respond. These were men who were to fight for their country but who were being shown that much of their country would not respect them as either soldiers or men. Colonel Hayward contacted the local press and asked them not to report the incident, and it was agreed that they would not. The black press, on the other hand, reported the incident and raised objections. The bulletin was brought up by the black press and pointed to as evidence that the commanding officers of the black soldiers were prejudiced. General Ballou complained that his motives were being misrepresented, that he had merely written a bulletin designed to make it easier for the black soldiers to avoid trouble.

On October 24, less than two weeks after they had arrived, the 15th was moved out of Spartanburg. They had missed valuable training, and many were feeling discouraged.

The army decided to ship the 15th to France immediately and continue their training abroad.

The men were glad to return to New York and eager to begin the adventure of traveling by ship to France. On November 11, 1917, they were taken to Hoboken, New Jersey, where the *Pocahontas*, an oceangoing transport ship, waited. That night, its lights darkened because of the fear of German submarines, the ship moved away from its pier. The men were finally on their way. Almost.

The next day the ship turned back with a damaged piston rod.

Instead of France, the men were now scheduled to go to Camp Merritt, near Cresskill, New Jersey.

At Camp Merritt the talk among the officers was about the Russian Revolution. The Bolsheviks had taken over the government and signed a treaty with Germany. The treaty would free German soldiers fighting against Russia on the eastern front. Military experts began predicting a major German offensive in the coming spring. To many, the economics of the war seemed to be forcing the conflict to an ending. The strains could be read in newspapers all across Europe.

In Great Britain factory workers were out on strike. Material shortages in France had already hurt the French army. But if things were bad in the factories, they were even worse in the homes. People across Europe were suffering from a scarcity of food. The United States Food Administration published the Hunger Map of Europe, showing famine conditions in eastern Europe, Russia, and Finland and serious conditions throughout the continent.

European newspapers asked, "Where are the Americans?" There was a growing sense of urgency for American fighting men to enter the war.

It took three weeks to repair the *Pocahontas*, but on December 2 the 15th was prepared to start again. There was one more mishap: The *Pocahontas* was struck on a foggy night by a British tanker. The damage was minor, but the *Pocahontas* needed repairs. The Navy men wanted to take it back to port for the repairs, but Hayward

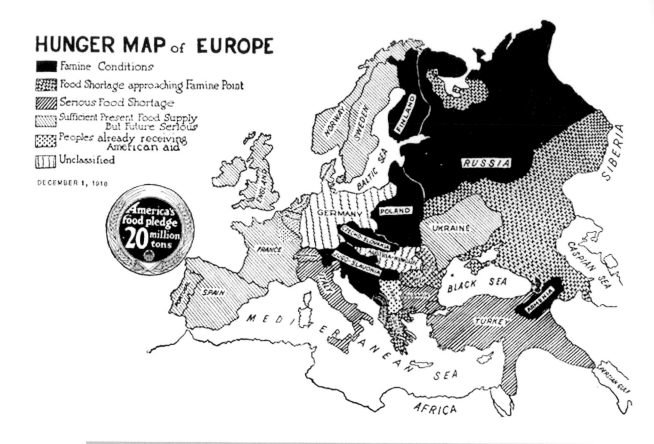

HUNGER MAP of EUROPE

■ Famine Conditions

▨ Food Shortage approaching Famine Point

▧ Serious Food Shortage

▨ Sufficient Present Food Supply
    But Future Serious

▨ Peoples already receiving
    American aid

▥ Unclassified

DECEMBER 1, 1918

America's food pledge **20** million tons

A desperate Europe

would have none of it and insisted it could be repaired at sea. It was, and the ship once again began its journey across the Atlantic.

On December 27 land was sighted. They had reached France. The men were confined to the ship until New Year's Day but were happy to be the first black unit to reach Europe.

CARRYING THE FLAG TO FRANCE

France! Few of the young men who made up the 15th had traveled far from their homes before entering the army. Now they were across the Atlantic Ocean in a place where the language was foreign, the sights were new, and even the color of their skin meant something different than it had in the United States. The band, with James Reese Europe as its head, was assigned to go on a goodwill mission to entertain French civilians. They went on a thirty-seven-day tour, playing for a war-weary population. Everywhere they went, they were well received. The band, made up of American blacks and Puerto Ricans, played music that the Europeans hadn't heard before.

At Nantes, Angers, and Tours the band was received with enthusiasm. These were the Americans, come to save a grateful France. At Chambéry they played for an orphans' home. At the conclusion of the outdoor concert James Reese Europe presented his baton to a young boy who had been watching and imitating him. The crowd, touched by the black man's humanity, applauded wildly.

But the 15th was not in France merely to be entertainers. And while the French did not discriminate on the basis of color, the American army still saw race as a problem.

The war in Europe had been dragging on for years with little advancement on either side. Both the Central Powers and the Allies were suffering from huge losses in manpower as well as food short-ages. French casualty lists ran as high as 70 percent killed or wounded. Now the Americans were bringing in shiploads of equipment and supplies, which would give the Allies a huge boost.

Most of the black soldiers, including members of the 15th, were being pressed into unloading the ships at Brest and other ports. The men began to complain. They had hoped for an opportunity to serve their country with courage and to prove their right to full citizenship, but now they were being reduced to common laborers. However, the need for labor and supplies was explained and the officers of the 15th, both black and white, emphasized the importance of getting the fresh equipment to the front lines.

But the men of the 15th did not want to be laborers. They had felt that the war would give them a chance to prove who they were as a people, and they wanted to participate in the upcoming battles. They were moved to a swampy area near Saint-Nazaire, south of

James Reese Europe and the 15th's band

Brest. There they saw hundreds of black soldiers cutting down trees and heavy vegetation, digging drainage ditches, and building roads. The fact that they were always being supervised by whites reminded some of the men of Southern chain gangs.

The War Department had created two black infantry divisions, the 92nd and the 93rd. The 15th, which had carried its National Guard colors into France, was assigned to the 93rd and later became

Unloading supplies at Brest

Assigned to Services of Supplies

the 369th Infantry Regiment. This reorganization into the regular Army was routinely done to maintain a consistent order.

General John "Black Jack" Pershing, head of the American Expeditionary Forces (AEF), had already offered to lend both black divisions to the Allies. He offered the 93rd to the French and the 92nd to the British. The British immediately refused the black soldiers. The French, desperate for manpower, accepted the offer.

In mid-March the negotiations between the French army and the

Americans were completed, and the unit from Harlem was officially assigned to the 16th French Division. The former 15th, now the 369th, continued to wear their American uniforms, but they were given French helmets, rifles, gas masks, and other gear.

Pershing had faced a dilemma. He knew that the basic motivation for the fighting man was the idea that he would be risking his life for his own country and for his loved ones back home. The American general had resisted the idea of having American soldiers fight under the French flag, but he also knew that if the French were going to continue to be an effective fighting force, they would need replacements. He was also aware of the discomfort that many of his officers felt about using black soldiers in combat. For the American government the issue of race relations was an important one, and the

With the French army in the trenches

War Department wanted to try to maintain the status quo at
home even if it meant some mistreatment of black soldiers overseas. This was in direct conflict with the expectations of many of
the soldiers and of the black population, who hoped that their
participation in the war would help bring an end to segregation
in the States.

No-man's-land

Later a French memo would be discovered showing the marked difference between the two nations. Entitled "Secret Information Concerning Black American Troops," it suggested that the French officers should not become too friendly with black officers: "We may be courteous and amiable with these last, but we cannot deal with them on the same plane as with the white American officers without deeply wounding the latter."

The letter was read in the French General Assembly after the war, much to the embarrassment of the French people. It was clear, however, that the source of the "instructions" was white American officers.

With the French army the 369th began its approach toward the war zone. The signs of combat were everywhere: the shells of buildings starkly silhouetted against the clear French sky; ruined vehicles, twisted and charred, by the sides of the roads; trees reduced to splinters; fields pockmarked with deep crevices made by explosives; the carcasses of dead animals; fences that once separated fruitful fields lying flat across the rolling landscape. And always, in the distance, the low rumble of artillery. The men, usually lighthearted, became deadly serious. They had wanted combat, and now they were headed toward the front lines. Thoughts of home flitted through the minds of men who previously were marveling only at the new land they were seeing. New cemeteries, the white crosses planted in neat rows like rigidly angled lilies, were constant reminders of the dangers that lay ahead.

As the men marched along the highways toward the front lines, seeing the devastation all around them, they had to wonder about their own lack of training. Combat infantry outfits normally train for four to five months before engaging an enemy. The 369th had had very little advanced training, none with their French weapons.

The men had to learn to use the French Lebel rifle, which was not nearly as good as the American Springfield. The American

officers also had to learn to communicate with their French counterparts, and an intensive training period began. The 369th was going to go into combat under the flag of officers most could not understand.

But the French soldiers treated them as equals, and with respect. French soldiers were assigned to work with the Americans to help them understand the difficulties they would be facing. The

Above: American cemetery in France. Right: Training with the French

The better part of valor.

Are you a brave man or a coward?

It takes a brave man to stand up for his principles. Cowards stand behind leaders and die, imagining that by so doing they become heroes.

The motive of an act is its measure. If you think the war is hell and that you as a citizen of the United States of America have no business to be fighting in France for England you are a coward to stay with it. If you had the courage to face criticism you would get out and over the top in no time to a place where there is some likelihood that you may see home again.

What business is this war in Europe to you anyhow? You don't want to annex anything, do you? You don't want to give up your life for the abstract thing «humanity».

If you believe in humanity and that life is precious, save your own life and dedicate it to the service of your own country and the woman who deserves it of you.

Lots of you fellows are staying with it because you are too cowardly to protest, to assert your own wills. Your wills are the best judges of what is best for you to do. Don't ask any one's opinion as to what you would better do! You know best what is the right thing to do. Do it and save your life! Germany never did any harm to you, all the newspaper tales of wrongs were printed to inflame you to the fighting pitch, they were lies, you know you can't believe what you read in the papers.

If you stay with the outfit ten chances to one, all you will get out of it will be a tombstone in France.

men from Harlem, in turn, put their hearts into the training. By mid-April, one month after they had been officially assigned to fight with the French army, the 369th was assigned a position near the Argonne Forest. They took more training at Maffrecourt, a relatively flat area that bore the marks of war. The distant booming of the big guns seemed very close, and occasionally the ground would shake with the impact of falling shells. The Germans were aware that the black soldiers were with the French. They dropped propaganda leaflets challenging their bravery or asking why, if they were treated so badly at home, they would fight to preserve the way of life that denigrated them.

The propaganda was ineffective. The men knew what fighting in the war meant to them and to the black race. Black journalists in Europe followed their every move and reported their successes and trials. Stories in the black press began to refer to the 369th as the Harlem Hellfighters.

The men of the 369th learned the French weapons quickly. They also met French colonial soldiers from Africa. The French officers were more than pleased with the Americans' discipline and relative good humor. But they also knew that the German troops coming from the eastern front would pose a severe challenge to the men, who had never experienced combat before. The Germans, to have

German propaganda

any chance to win the war, would have to strike quickly, before the Americans gained experience. Rumors of a major German offensive turned into a surety as intelligence reports showed a hurried buildup along the entire western front. The offensive would be on French territory in the spring. If the black troops held in battle, they could save France.

11

ON THE LINE

By mid-April 1918 the 369th was placed in position along the defensive line that stretched across France, waiting for the German push. There had been brief skirmishes, and the men were getting used to the tensions of combat. Enemy artillery fire had plowed up the ground around the trenches, and the 369th had experienced its first casualties. They were even used to the German spotter planes, marked with the German cross, that flew over their lines taking photographs as they remained tantalizingly out of the reach of small-arms fire. Besides the planes searching out their positions, there were also German patrols probing for weaknesses along the lines. The German soldiers were disciplined and daring, Needham Roberts, from Trenton, New Jersey, and Henry Johnson, from Albany, New York, were to find out.

Henry Johnson was born in Alexandria, Virginia, around 1895.

Henry Johnson

His family was poor, and it was all that his mother could do to keep her family fed. The family went south to live with relatives shortly after Henry was born, settling in Winston-Salem, North Carolina. This small, largely rural community offered little more than backbreaking farmwork for any uneducated man, black or white. At five foot four and barely 130 pounds, Johnson was not considered to be a good prospect even as a farmhand, the prevalent work in the area. In his teens he joined the thousands of other young black men who headed north, unsure of what they would find in the big cities but knowing they were not leaving much behind.

When Johnson arrived in Albany, the capital of New York state, his prospects were not good. So when he found a job at the busy railroad station as a porter, he was pleased. There was very little actual pay for the porters, but if they were lucky, the tips might be good. Johnson worked at the station, and when things were slow there, he worked in a combination drugstore and soda shop, mixing sodas.

Eventually he met a woman, a minister's daughter, and fell in love. In 1915, when Johnson was about twenty, the young couple was married and settled on Monroe Street in downtown Albany.

Marriage can be difficult for anyone, but for a young man without an education the pressures can be unbearable. Still, Johnson had to do the best he could. Part of that "best" was understanding the world around him. He knew that there was a major war taking place in Europe and, in 1917, knew that a number of his friends were joining a black National Guard regiment being formed in New York City. He thought it was his duty to join. He was assigned to Company C of the 15th, later the 369th.

Needham Roberts worked as a store clerk in Trenton, New Jersey. A handsome, well-spoken young man, he yearned for more adventure than the small shop offered. The new black regiment being formed in New York sounded like such an adventure. Being in the army during wartime would be dangerous, of course, but it would also be a chance to see a foreign land and to discover more about himself. The trip from Trenton to Harlem took a little less than two hours, but as he boarded the train, Roberts knew that it would probably be the most important trip of his life. It was a trip that would soon bring him to the adventure of his life in the Argonne Forest.

The Argonne Forest lies between two rivers in northeastern France, the Meuse and the Aisne. On this heavily wooded plateau the Germans had built a strong defensive position, which the French had not been able to successfully penetrate. On May 13, 1918, Henry Johnson and Needham Roberts, both in Company C, were on guard duty in forward posts.

The main guard post was stationed on the outer edge of the 1st Battalion's position, several hundred yards from where the companies were bedded down for the night. Johnson and Roberts were sixty yards forward of that. It was a dangerous spot, and they knew it as they waited in the darkness. Pieces of tin had been attached to the barbed-wire fencing, and they listened for any sound of the tin being disturbed.

Time passed slowly. It was early morning when they heard the first sounds. Were they voices? And where were they coming from? Neither man wore a watch, but both knew that it was too early for their relief. They heard the voices again and realized that they were closer than they had first thought, and that they were unmistakably German.

They moved apart, as they had been trained to do. No sense in letting a lucky German burst of fire get both of them. They wondered where their relief was. Johnson took the hand grenades from his service bag and carefully laid them on the ground in front of his position. His palms were wet, and he wiped them on his pants. More time passed, and the area was quiet.

Johnson leaned his rifle carefully against the tree a half arm's length away. He touched the bolo knife that hung from his belt and loosed the string that tied it to his leg. The heavy bolo knife had come from an African soldier. The white French soldiers had laughed when they saw some members of the 369th trade with the Senagalese soldiers for the weapons, but Johnson noticed that no one started an argument with the African troops.

The thought came to him that perhaps the voices had just been a passing German patrol. He knew the Germans were aware of the Allied soldiers and probably knew exactly where their trenches were. He tensed as he listened for new sounds. Each rustle of the wind, each chirping of any of the thousands of creatures that lived in the forest had the ring of danger.

Needham Roberts

The moon drifted easily through the distant clouds, sending uneven slivers of light between the dark silhouettes of the trees. Suddenly there was a rapid series of clicks. Johnson held his breath and listened as hard as he could. Then he recognized the sound. Wire cutters! The Germans were cutting their way through the barbed wire!

Both men grabbed for their grenades and began tossing them.

The French rifle, the Lebel, was not known for its accuracy, but in the dark of night Johnson couldn't see anything clearly anyway. He fired as many shots as he could, reloading the three-shot magazine and jerking off shots until the gun jammed.

By that time the Germans had completely cut through the barbed wire, and he could see their forms closing in on him. He swung the eight-and-a-half-pound weapon with all his strength. Powerful arms grabbed at the rifle and pulled while another arm reached around his neck.

Johnson felt himself being pulled backward as he freed his bolo knife from its makeshift sling. He swung the bolo knife down at the leg of the soldier who held him. The German howled in pain and released his grip on Johnson's neck. Quickly stepping to one side, Johnson swung wildly in front of him, keeping the edge of the sharply curved knife always above his waist, as he had seen the Africans do.

For a moment he was clear, and then he heard German voices to his right. Even in the semidarkness he could see that they were trying to drag someone away. It was Roberts!

The 369th had sworn among themselves not to be captured or to lose their men to the enemy. They prided themselves on fighting to the end. Johnson, filled with an almost desperate rage, rushed across the short distance and attacked the retreating Germans. In the darkness the Germans weren't sure of what they were facing or how many. They just knew that they were being sliced up badly and that even the man on the ground was fighting furiously. They released Roberts just as more men from the 369th, alerted by the sounds of fighting, arrived. The Germans fired their Mausers as they retreated quickly through the barbed wire.

Both Henry Johnson and Needham Roberts were badly wounded in the battle. Johnson had been shot three times and had numerous bayonet wounds. Roberts was also badly wounded and had lost a lot of blood. But the Germans had not broken through. Forty grenades, seven pairs of wire cutters, and a number of weapons were found as daylight brightened the area. From the amount of blood found in the tracks of the retreating German patrol, the French investigators concluded that at least four of the enemy soldiers had been fatally wounded, and perhaps as many as a dozen injured. The wounded had been lucky to escape with their lives in the ferocious battle.

In recognition of their efforts, both Henry Johnson and Needham Roberts received the Croix de Guerre, the highest award the French army gives for valor and heroism in battle. There were no American awards given.

The accounts of Johnson's feats were all written by his white officers. As such they were universally given a humorous twist. Johnson's dialogue was carefully scripted to show that he was not an educated man, and his replies were milked, and probably written for

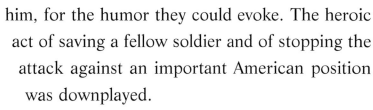

him, for the humor they could evoke. The heroic act of saving a fellow soldier and of stopping the attack against an important American position was downplayed.

But the men of the 369th appreciated what Johnson and Roberts had done. Although they had both been badly wounded, they had faced the Germans and taken them on in hand-to-hand combat. And they had prevailed.

Left: Henry Johnson. Above: Croix de Guerre

THE GERMAN OFFENSIVE

The years of trench warfare, in which neither side gained significant advantage, were draining the Allies of men and morale. The addition of the American troops and supplies had been desperately needed but did not provide the kinds of strategic wins that General Pershing thought would end the war. And American soldiers attacking entrenched German forces suffered major casualties even when they were deemed successful. The war could have settled down again into the bloody trench maneuvers that had marked the first three years, but the Central Powers were running out of supplies on the front lines, and Germans were suffering much more than people living in the faraway British and American cities. But the Germans, who were now directing the Austrian army as well as their own, had signed a treaty with

Russia in March and now were bringing men from the eastern front to face the Allies in the west.

The men of the 369th were told of the coming offensive. The French felt that the next few months would be a turning point in the war.

The constant shelling, the gas attacks, and the German snipers were taking their toll on the men from Harlem. In Maffrecourt a corner of one cemetery was dedicated to the black Americans who had lost their lives so far from home.

The battalions of the 369th took turns manning the trenches as they readied themselves for the assault to come. German planes flew over their positions, sometimes dropping bombs, sometimes just photographing the fortifications. The officers worried about the replacements being sent from the States. Most of them were young black men who had been farmers and who had been drafted into the Army. They had had little military training, if any, before being sent as replacements for those killed and wounded. The major qualification of some of the new men was that they were black and so were routinely sent to a black outfit. They had to be trained in the trenches, and if they were lucky, they lived long enough to learn how to defend themselves.

June passed by slowly, with the Germans constantly testing the French and American forces. Night after night the trenches were hit with deadly gas attacks and high-explosive shells. General Henri

The soldiers traveled in boxcars (the sign indicates the car holds 32–40 men or 8 horses lengthwise)

Gouraud, the commanding French general, had high praise for the black troops under his command. On July 7, 1918, he wrote a memorandum about the impending assault.

ORDER

TO THE FRENCH AND AMERICAN SOLDIERS OF THE 4TH ARMY.

We may be attacked now at any moment.

You all feel that never was a defensive battle engaged under more favorable conditions.

We are informed and we are ready.

We are powerfully reinforced in infantry and in artillery.

We fight on a ground you have transformed by your persistent work into a formidable fortress—an invincible fortress if all the passages are well guarded.

The bombardment will be terrible; you will bear it without flagging.

The assault will be severe, in a cloud of dust, of smoke, and of gas. . . .

In your breasts beat brave and strong hearts of free men. Nobody will look back, nobody will fall back one step.

Everybody will have but one thought: Kill, kill many until they have had enough of it.

This is why your general tells you: You will break their assault. It will be a beautiful day.

GOURAUD

The attack came at midnight on July 14. It was Bastille Day, the day the French celebrate the fall of the notorious prison and the transformation of their country into a republic.

It began with a thunderous artillery duel as far as the men could see, at least fifty miles to either side of them. As the shells pounded the ground around them, the men took whatever shelter they could find in the second trenches. At each lull they would have to pop up out of the trenches to see if the German infantry was headed their way.

At last the artillery did stop, and through the smoke and gas-filled air the first wave of German infantry came.

The French officers pulled the men back from the front trenches and zeroed their artillery on the abandoned trenches, turning them into killing zones. The desperate Germans forced their way out of the first trench lines and struggled toward the heavily fortified second lines, at a great loss of men and equipment.

The battle raged from night into morning, and still the guns roared and men threw themselves across the open fields. The Germans sustained the staggering losses typical of a charging army and slowly began to retreat. The Allied line had held against the first assault. But it was just the first. The artillery fire started instantly, and the combat intensified. On July 16 Corporal Horace Pippin's life changed forever.

Horace Pippin was born on February 22, 1888, in West Chester, Pennsylvania. By the age of ten he had moved with his mother to Goshen, New York. His early life was typical of that of many young

Artillery fire leads the charge

black boys: He dropped out of school in his early teens and began a life as a common laborer. At fifteen he was doing the backbreaking work of unloading coal from freight cars. In 1912, after the death of his mother, he worked in Paterson, New Jersey. In 1916 he was working in Mahwah, New Jersey, as a molder.

Pippin had always been interested in art and had attracted some attention in his church community for his crayon drawings as a child. A tall man of exceptional physical strength, Pippin had a keen interest in the folk stories he heard and often tried to draw pictures illustrating the stories.

In the black community there have always been "race men,"

black males whose interests centered on the advancement of the black race. There have also been men who seemed to represent the best of the black male aspect, who constantly served as the strength of the community. Pippin was such a man. When the United States declared war on Germany in March 1917, Pippin remembered the colored regiment being formed in New York and enlisted.

Pippin was twenty-nine at the time of his enlistment and, like most Americans, had little idea of what war was about. But the rigors of training were apparently to his liking, and when he was assigned to Camp Dix, New Jersey, he took to it with gusto. It was at Camp Dix that he made corporal, which meant that he had some-how managed to distinguish himself from the other volunteers.

In a brief biography by Judith Stein, *I Tell My Heart*, Pippin talks of the month he trained with the French to learn their weapons and their systems of fighting. He mentions going into combat at Bois-d'Hauze and the shock of being in a war zone.

When the Germans started their attack in July, the French command wanted to know as much as possible about it. They sent out patrols to capture prisoners from whom they hoped to get information. It was a dangerous mission, and Pippin knew it when he left the American-held trench.

The small squad of French and black American soldiers was to make its way to the forward trenches, then go through no-man's-land toward the enemy position, capture a German soldier, and return as quickly and as safely as possible. The Germans, of course, were waiting and prepared for just such an attempt.

A few yards out of the trench Pippin and the men with him were pinned down by German machine-gun fire. Pippin believed in himself and thought the mission would still succeed. But he soon felt a searing blow to his right arm that knocked him to the ground. A German sniper had got him. The pain was excruciating, and Pippin fought not to pass out. A French soldier came to the ditch in which Pippin was lying and tried to assess the situation. Pippin signaled for the Frenchman to get down, but before the man could react, a bullet tore through his forehead. The startled soldier seemed frozen for a moment, then fell lifelessly beside Pippin. Slowly, painfully, Pippin made his way back to the safety of the French trenches. His war was over.

The nerves in his arm were torn apart, the muscles severed by the sniper's bullet. Pippin would not be able to move his right arm for years to come. But eventually he would move the arm and tell the story, in pictures and words, of what it was like to fight in a war, and what it was like to fight that war as a black man.

Pippin's drawings of the war were moving and stark. His depictions of war are free from romanticism and fully expressive of the pain and horror of what he had experienced as a soldier in the 369th.

IN ENEMY HANDS

The 161st French Division, with which the 369th also fought, moved along the line from Maffrecourt to Minaucourt, some twenty-five miles westward. The area had already seen years of fighting and hundreds of thousands of casualties.

As the 369th advanced into position, they were raked with artillery fire and took heavy casualties. But by the end of July it was the attacking German divisions that had retreated, leaving thousands of young, and equally brave, German soldiers scattered over the fields. The war was devastating for both sides, with heroes being made by necessity.

"Our father, Don, was with the medical unit," Ann and Jeni Estill told me. "He didn't carry a gun but wore a white armband, which should have protected him. But when he went out in no-man's-land to bring in a wounded soldier, he was the one they shot at first.

"He told us of a time when he and another private ran out into the open, lifted a soldier who had been badly wounded on a stretcher, and started back to the French-American lines. They hadn't gone but a few feet when his partner was killed. Daddy dragged the stretcher as the wounded man held on for dear life. Somehow they made it back safely."

Many times neither the wounded nor those trying to help them made it back to the safety of the trenches. The losses of the 369th grew larger each day. So did its pride.

For the next month the French and the Americans pushed the Germans slowly backward, with both sides taking considerable losses. The 369th was gassed a number of times, and the constant fighting was taking a toll on morale. But the German prisoners— and there were thousands being captured—were equally despondent. The 369th had not lost any of its men as prisoners, although there had been close calls.

On the night of August 17, 1918, a small group of soldiers from the 369th was in the frontline trenches, unable to move back to the safer reserve trenches due to the intensity of the shelling. Then there was a lull in the shelling, and the men considered moving back when they suddenly found themselves surrounded by a German squad.

They were quickly disarmed and hustled forward, prodded by the muzzles of the Germans' pistols. As they stumbled forward through the darkness, they neared a concealed Allied listening post. Inside the post was Sergeant William Butler, of Salisbury, Maryland. A

slight, soft-spoken man, Butler had done odd jobs before joining the army. He had adapted well to the discipline and rigors of army life and had raised himself to the position of sergeant.

Butler allowed the Germans and their black prisoners to come near enough for him to see them clearly. He quickly devised a plan that, while putting his own life in danger, would have the best chance of rescuing the members of his company. If he attacked hard enough, and with enough ferocity, he could take advantage of the darkness and the confusion of combat. He took a deep breath, shouted a warning, and opened fire.

The Germans, knowing that they were in the vicinity of the black Americans and not knowing how many they were facing, began an immediate withdrawal. Butler allowed the men from the 369th a few seconds to disengage themselves from the Germans before he opened

fire again. How many Germans were killed by Butler is uncertain, but because of him the 369th's record of never losing a man as a prisoner was intact. He was yet another hero of the regiment.

With the failure of the German offensive in the summer of 1918, the outcome of the war was certain. The Allies had fresh American soldiers and were being backed by an American economy that hadn't been drained by years of supporting the war effort. Still, the German

Casualties mounted quickly

military would not concede defeat. As the fighting continued, diplomats on both sides began tentative discussions of terms for a surrender as the fighting went on. The war that had already seen millions killed, and had caused so much suffering, continued to claim victims.

The Germans, at this point in the conflict, knew that they could not win the war. Their only hope was to strengthen their position at the peace talks. The Central Powers had been the aggressors and reasoned that the Allies would demand a high price to stop the bloodshed.

THE BATTLE OF
MEUSE-ARGONNE

September 1918

he Allied offensive in the Meuse-Argonne region was designed to push the Germans back beyond their forward supply lines. The 369th Infantry, still attached to the French, would be a vital part of that push. Arthur Little, now a major, received orders to move the 1st Battalion into position. All along the front it was the Allies who were on the offensive, and they were taking a great many casualties. To the north the 372nd was engaged in heavy fighting and losing a lot of men.

The Germans had retreated, abandoning the trenches they had occupied. Some German positions had been quickly overrun by forward troops, and the men of the 369th saw a stream of enemy prisoners being taken into Allied lines. The prisoners looked tired and weary of war.

The land between the forces had been ripped up by years of artillery bombardment, which made pushing the heavy cannons almost impossible. Mules, horses, and men were used to nudge the huge guns forward through the heavy mud. There were trenches to go over, plus miles of barbed wire, much of it hidden in the mud, and the bodies of the dead.

The trenches were particularly dangerous, for the Germans knew exactly where they were and could zero their artillery with amazing accuracy on the twisting lines. Major Little found the bodies of a dozen men from the 2nd Battalion who had taken an enemy trench only to be killed when the shelling began. Still, his men moved forward.

The 1st Battalion was in the third wave of attackers, just out of range of the small-arms fire but subjected to the heavy shells of the cannons.

September 28

During the early hours the 2nd Battalion attacked the ridge at Bellevue Signal along with two French battalions. They took the ridge, but at an enormous cost. The wounded were being carried back through the lines to get what medical treatment they could. When it was possible, the dead were buried in shallow graves, with the hope that their bodies would later be recovered.

The 1st Battalion was due to move to the front lines. On the twenty-eighth they sat in whatever cover they could find and endured the steady rain. Their tents were made in two halves, with wooden pins to fasten them to the ground. The men took the halves and pinned them down over narrow portions of trenches to keep as much of the rain out as possible.

Looking across no-man's-land toward the enemy

September 29

The 1st Battalion moved up to the Bellevue Signal Ridge and relieved a French unit. After assembling in the grim darkness of the early morning, they checked their equipment and prepared to go over the top. Their orders were to move toward and take the town of Sechault.

Sechault is a small town with neat, multistoried houses laid out in straight rows. It was surrounded by relatively flat land that would not conceal their movements. Major Little knew that the Germans had occupied the city and were ready to defend it. The enemy would know the layout of Sechault better than the men of the 369th and would have a plan of defense ready. If the 369th could take the city, the cost would be high. But Little had been given orders to do exactly that, and as day began to break, the Harlem fighters moved out.

Silhouetted against the sunlight, they soon came under enemy artillery fire. The flat lands surrounding the town were a nightmare. The men, crouching low and running as quickly as they could under the weight of their equipment, could only pray that they would not be hit by artillery shells.

Once within the town's borders the men began working their way through the streets. Heavy machine guns often have a range of more than a mile. The German machine gunners aimed their weapons down the relatively wide avenues of Sechault, daring any man to cross them. Soldiers began to time the firing as the guns sprayed death from side to side.

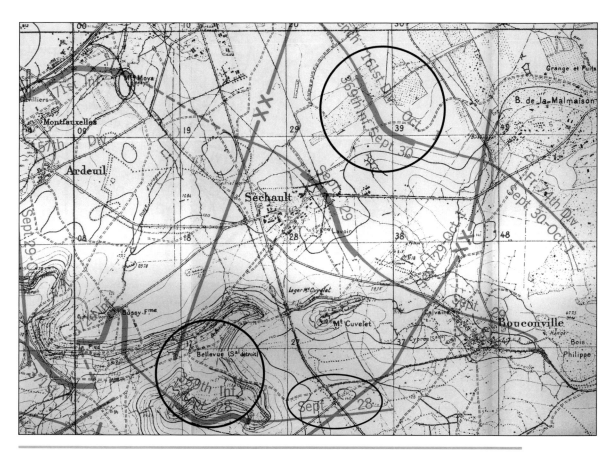

Combat map showing position of the 369th

The fighting raged all day, with the men of the 369th measuring their success through the town in yards. There were Germans in the town itself, left to defend their positions or die.

As the evening wore on, a German plane circled overhead, diving now and again to spot the positions of the invading battalions. A number of the 1st Battalion's officers had been wounded. Scouts reported that the 2nd Battalion was down to about half strength, and enemy activity at the north end of the town might mean a counter-attack.

Night fell swiftly. Sechault was dark except for burning buildings here and there. The town was still being raked by machine-gun fire and artillery shells; the constant booming of the big guns and the subsequent explosions continued into the night. The Germans sent up flares. First there would be the silent, dim trace of a glowing object as it headed high over the town; then there would be the explosion of the flare into a brilliant light arcing across the dark sky, making the area below almost daylight bright for several seconds before the flare fell to the ground. Each time a flare went up, the men would look down to keep the light from reflecting off their faces.

That night the Germans didn't know if the men had stayed in the town or had retreated. The 369th had moved into a series of irregular trenches around the town to avoid the pinpoint accuracy of the German guns. Major Little told his men to resist firing into the darkness, to keep their positions hidden.

The Germans remaining in Sechault, as well as the Americans, were within the gun sights of German machine gunners firing from as much as a mile away. But slowly, methodically, the men of the 369th silenced the guns within the town. It was September 30.

Dozens of men lay dead or wounded, thousands of miles from home, in a town whose name few knew even as they attacked. The battalion was now at less than two-thirds strength. Just beyond Sechault several companies were trying to push their way into the

The cost of war

Argonne Forest. The Germans were masters of defending wooded
areas, and from the hastily set up command post on the edge of
Sechault the German machine-gun fire could be seen flashing like
angry fireflies through the trees. There were instant reports of even
more casualties, and Major Little commanded his men to retreat. He

called for supporting artillery fire, knowing it would do little good in the heavily bunkered woods.

The Allies sent up observation balloons. Major Little described what happened to one of them: "One day a Boche [German] plane

came over, pounced down out of a cloud, set fire to our observation balloon, shot and killed with machine guns the poor observer who leaped from the flaming balloon and was peacefully descending in his parachute. This Boche scoundrel then came still lower and

Burying the dead

darted over our headquarters so low that some of the men threw stones at him, having no time to run and get rifles which were a few rods away."

The 369th pushed forward, and no man present could escape witnessing the carnage. Major Little reported the results of the attack:

"There were many gruesome sights continually before us. I noticed that our men and the French, when killed, generally cuddled up in a heap. The Boche, however, was all sprawled out. Maybe because we were always attacking and most of the time crouched down. . . . We crossed a small cemetery, used until a few weeks before the attack by the civilian community. Our artillery and theirs had pounded this spot

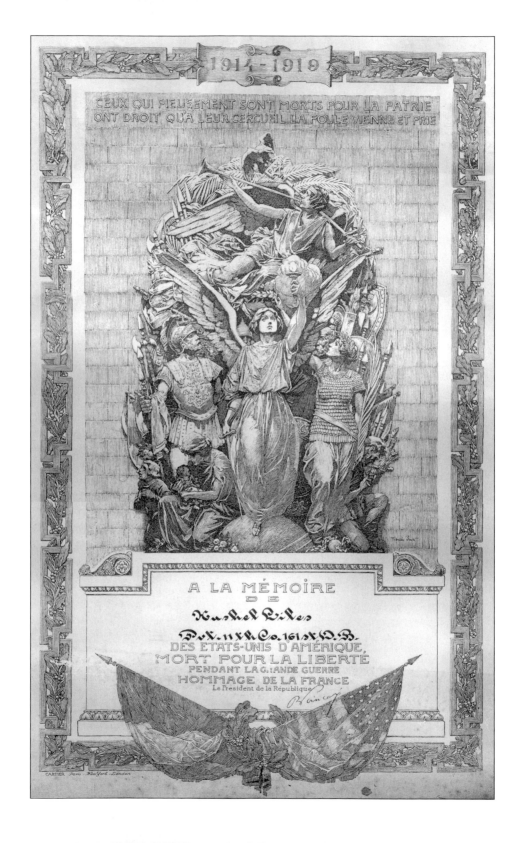

until the graves were literally blown out of the spot."

After the attack on Sechault and the first bloody assault on the forests west of the city, Major Little was informed that the attack had been a success and was asked to resume the assault. The major looked around at the wounded men being treated and the bodies being stacked for burial. He felt sick at the loss of life around him.

Yes, they would advance if ordered, Little replied; but he felt the cost would be extremely high and said as much in his message.

The barrage by the big guns continued until evening, when the men were ordered to cease the attack. The killing had stopped for the day.

The fighting continued through all of October, with both sides aware that it would soon be over. The 369th moved to the Vosges Mountains, a few miles from the German border, to prepare for the next attack. They were shelled daily, but sustained few casualties until the twenty-eighth of the month, when four men were killed and eight more wounded.

The men were tired. Many of their friends—their fellow soldiers, black and white—had been killed and buried in shallow graves throughout France. But they had triumphed. They had been part of the Allied force that had defeated the mighty German army. Needham Roberts and Henry Johnson had been awarded the Croix de Guerre. The entire 369th had also won the

The French commemorate American dead

French award as a fighting unit.

They had come from the streets of New York, from Trenton, from Albany. They had been nearly invisible as porters and clerks and factory workers. Now the entire world knew who they were. They were the black heroes of the 15th, the Harlem Hellfighters.

On November 11, all the rumors and press reports proved to be true. An armistice had been declared; the fighting had ended.

The 369th marched proudly into Germany. They were victors in an unbelievably bloody

Above: Don V. Estill (circled) plays clarinet with the James Reese Europe Band

Right: Harlem Hellfighters

and useless war. None of the designs of the aggressors had been successful; more than ten million humans had lost their lives, and countless more would suffer for decades to come.

But the men from Harlem had shown their bravery, their patriotism, and their abilities. As they marched through the streets of Germany and France, and the band under James Reese Europe played American melodies to crowds weary of war, they knew what

they had done, and were proud of their accomplishments both as African Americans and as men.

Don V. Estill, who had served as a medic and spent much of the war dashing through no-man's-land, avoiding instant death, now joined Europe's band as a musician. He was thankful for the end of the killing and, finally, the end of the war.

15

THE PARADE

As the men of the 369th returned from the front, there was no mistaking what they had accomplished. They had confronted the enemy and had prevailed. And they had done so without losing a man to the enemy as a prisoner and without giving up an inch of ground. They were the Harlem Hellfighters.

In a small town in France a white American military policeman saw French girls kissing the black soldiers and ordered the men, who had been marching in casual formation through the town, back into the middle of the street.

"Who won the war?" the soldiers asked. "Who won the war?"

The Allies had won the war, and the 369th had been an integral part of that effort. They had fought and bled and died in the woods and the fields and the towns of France. If the world was now safe for democracy, they had helped make it so.

"Who won the war?" they asked again.

The 369th arrived at Camp Pontanezen, which was used as an embarkation camp, in mid-January. The men were tired, their job was finished; but for two weeks they were given petty labor jobs, once again reduced to doing service jobs while white troops waiting for embarkation relaxed. The company officers knew the men were on edge and

warned them not to mar their record at this late date, and they didn't. Finally the orders came for them to leave, and on January 31, 1919, they marched to the pier. James Reese Europe's band played as the

Left: Soldiers were welcomed by the French

Below: Salvation Army workers with the troops

Above: James Reese Europe and band headed for home. Right: Black soldiers—triumphant!

men boarded the small boats that brought them to the ships that would take them home.

On February 17, 1919, the 369th was in parade formation on Twenty-third Street in New York City. At eleven o'clock in the morning Colonel Hayward gave the order the men had been waiting for.

"Forward, march!"

They marched up Fifth Avenue from Twenty-third Street. Thousands of cheering

Top: Proud spectators. Bottom and right: Parade in New York City

New Yorkers on their lunch hour filled the sidewalks and applauded wildly as the soldiers marched past them.

The entertainer Bill "Bojangles" Robinson marched with them for a part of the way. The band played, and the men marched smartly in the bright sunlight. Then they reached Harlem.

Left: Harlem celebrates its young heroes. Below: Harlem was so proud

Children welcome the marchers

They had fought for the country's pride and for their own, for world democracy and for their own share of it. Now they marched proudly through the streets from which many of them had come. Harlemites were cheering, and some were crying. Wounded vets, some with missing limbs, saluted as their fellow soldiers passed.

When James Reese Europe and his band started playing the popular song "Here Comes My Daddy Now," people began to break into the ranks and hug their sons and husbands. As Major Little remarked in his book, *From Harlem to the Rhine*: "It was a regiment of men, who had done the work of men."

It was a day of triumph, a moment of glory that would remain in the hearts of Harlemites for years to come.

16

RED SUMMER

World War I was a war of hopelessly muddled causes rooted in the imperialism of the past and with no clear victory for any of the combatants. In January 1918, President Woodrow Wilson had delivered a speech in which he outlined Fourteen Points that would have to be agreed to for a lasting peace if all nations were to have a hope of living in an atmosphere of self-determination and unfettered sovereignty. But these were quickly cast aside in favor of the narrow interests of the victors. Germany was reduced both physically and economically and saddled with enormous debts. Japan took advantage of its wartime military preparedness to take over Chinese territory. Many colonial soldiers who had helped the Allies win the war found themselves stranded far from home and unrewarded for their efforts.

American soldiers returned home with the same hopes as all the

W A R   D E P A R T M E N T

WASHINGTON.

March 13, 1919.

MEMORANDUM FOR CAPTAIN ELLIOT P. FROST,
Morale Branch, General Staff,
War Department.

I wish to thank you for calling to my attention that paragraph (#11) of the accompanying memoranda, returned herewith, which bears upon the employment of colored soldiers who have returned from overseas and the seeming tendency on the part of quite a number of them to flock to the northern states, etc. I have made careful note of this portion of the report submitted, and for sometime I have been giving considerable thought to the matter above referred to with a view to working out some plan or at least making some definite suggestions designed to encourage and bring about the employment of an increased number of returning colored soldiers in occupations and sections of the country that woudl be of most benefit to themselves and most helpful in the reconstruction period. I have several conferences now pending bearing upon this whole matter, and I hope soon to be able to suggest (at his request, to Col. Arthur H. Woods, Special Asst., etc.), how the War Department may help, either directly or indirectly, in obtaining the desired result.

Sincerely yours,

Emmett J. Scott,
Special Assistant to Secretary of War,
Rooms 144,146, War Department.

3 Enclosures.
WHD

Emmett J. Scott replies to concerns on black migration

victors. They wanted to be lauded, to have their sacrifices appreciated. But they were returning to a changing nation. The United States was moving away from its agricultural roots and becoming more and more industrialized. Both blacks and whites were leaving the South and heading toward Northern cities.

America had become a great industrial power, but the economy was changing rapidly. The farms that had supported much of the population were now suffering as prices dropped in America and exports to Europe also dropped. As the northern factories switched from war production to civilian products, jobs became scarce. Returning white soldiers found themselves competing for jobs against blacks. A number of race riots broke out across the United States. The root causes of the riots were the same issues that America had been dealing with during the war: What was to be the role of blacks in American life?

The Anatomy of a Race Riot

Race riots are often caused by small, seemingly insignificant events, such as a rumor that someone was attacked or was threatened by another group. Sometimes an incident involving a personal dispute between two people can escalate into a general riot. In Chicago a black youth swimming in a pool was the target of stones thrown by one or more white youths. The black, not a good swimmer, drowned. In the ensuing riot thirty-eight people were killed, fifteen whites and twenty-three blacks. Five hundred people were

Statement

Chicago, November 3, 1919.

The people of the City of Chicago should be informed of the true facts of the Race Riot, especially as to the number who lost their lives, in order that false rumors may be set at rest and the good name of the City of Chicago be redeemed.

As many people believe, in and out of the city, that thousands were killed and the facts suppressed from the public, I, Peter M. Hoffman, Coroner, do hereby certify under oath and the official seal of my office that the total number of deaths due to Race Rioting in the City of Chicago for the year 1919 number thirty-eight (38), fifteen (15) whites, and twenty-three (23) colored.

Riots of Red Summer

injured. In Washington, D.C., a riot left 40 dead and 150 wounded. Many black men were lynched that year. Some of them were veterans of the war still in their uniforms. There were so many deaths and so much bloodshed during the hot months of 1919 that it was called Red Summer.

What they found upon their return from the war was disappointing to the black men who had fought for their country, including the men of the 369th, but they had had experiences that would change their lives forever. In many ways the war changed all of black America. The war, and the participation of the Harlem Hellfighters against a skilled and determined enemy, demonstrated that courage and bravery and heroism knew no color lines. They were all Americans.

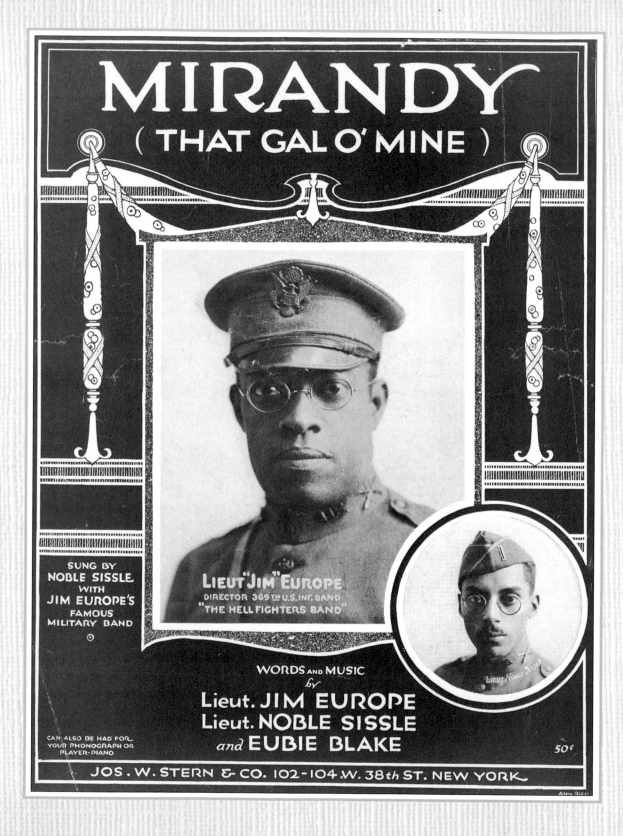

17

HEROES AND MEN

T he story of the Harlem Hellfighters is not simply one of victory in a war. Indeed, it is not even one of unexpected courage, amazing feats, or a disregard for danger. The men suffered when one would have expected them to suffer, they fell wounded when hit by shrapnel or bullets, and many of them died. But it is the story of men who acted as men, and who gave good accounts of themselves when so many people thought, even hoped, that they would fail.

When the soldiers of the 15th New York National Guard boarded the ships that would take them to France, they took with them the hopes and dreams of an entire people. They were in the prayers of black congregations throughout the nation each Sunday morning,

James Europe sheet music

and in the thoughts and dreams of thousands of black families.

Those who died in the trenches and amid the barbed wire did so upholding the dignity of their race and of their country. They had fought for their country, and they had proved, beyond doubt, that they had a right to fight. Those who returned to march through the streets of New York, who paraded uptown past the cheering Harlem crowds, did so as heroes. They had helped to make the world safe for democracy and had held the banner of black dignity high enough for all the world to see.

Many had hoped their sacrifices would make a change in how America saw them. They had hoped that the derogatory terms so casually tossed at them by bigots would be discarded once the first man of them went over the top. In this effort, even the Harlem Hellfighters were not successful.

But the men who rose from those trenches after hours of shelling, who climbed the hills and waded through the mud, who rushed across no-man's-land with bayonets pointed at the enemy, would forever be heroes to their community, and to all Americans who understood what they had accomplished.

Carrying the spoils of war

SELECTED BIBLIOGRAPHY

Badger, Reid. *A Life in Ragtime: A Biography of James Reese Europe*. New York: Oxford University Press, 1995.

Barbeau, Arthur E., and Florette Henri. *The Unknown Soldiers: African American Troops in World War I*. New York: Da Capo Press, 1996.

Center of Military History. *United States Army in the World War*, Volume 3. Washington: Center of Military History, 1989.

Harris, Steven L. *Harlem's Hell Fighters: The African-American 369th Infantry in World War I*. Washington: Brassey's, Inc., 2003.

Little, Arthur W. *From Harlem to the Rhine: The Story of New York's Colored Volunteers*. New York: Covici, Friede, 1936.

A Pictorial History of the Negro in the Great World War, 1917–1918. New York: Toussaint Pictorial Company, Inc., 1931.

Scott, Emmett Jay. *Scott's Official History of the American Negro in the World War.* Chicago: Homewood, 1919.

Stein, Judith. *I Tell My Heart: The Art of Horace Pippin*. New York: Pennsylvania Academy of Fine Arts, 1993.

On the Web

U.S. National Archives & Records Administration (NARA): http://www.archives.gov/education/lessons/369th-infantry/

Interview: Ann and Jeni Estill